— Sir Knight Writes-

I0098207

My Mirrors Reflection

Inner Selfs Journal Journey On

#LoveOn

J. Sir Knight

www.jonathandekle.com Via Contact Us

ISBN: 0692777199
ISBN-13: 978-0692777190

Thank You

L ive On

O ne Love God

V alue Life

E veryday Counts

O ver power Negativity

N ever give up

#LoveOnForever
#LoveOn
#HeartVibes
#LoveVibes
#PositiveVibes

DEDICATION

Here's to those who have had depression. Who have felt the world against them the most. Who have faced demons in their lives. Who struggle through spirituality. This book is a reflection of such. It's a battle to try to become someone better, to understand life and why we are here clearer. May these words inspire and bless you with understanding; letting you know you do not stand alone in this world faced with such hardships. Here is my mirrors reflection. May it enlighten you to know that darkness surely is a part of this life, but so is light!

I express my past here in a way that is as expressive as I know how too.
Talk about what I personally have been through, What conversations go on in my thoughts—
How I used to think and express life,
Diving in between past, present and future reflections of myself. Leaving you to say at the end of the day which reflection you really see. May these words only help inspire you to know, We all have crazy thoughts,
We all have been in bad places. We all are much a like, yet we all have our own perspectives that only words and expressions can help us understand better, so we can understand life easier.

*OTHER PUBLISHED WORKS BY **JONATHAN DEKLE**
AVAILABLE VIA **AMAZON***

MAGNIFICENT LOVE: THE END REALLY THE BEGINNING

||

MAGNIFICENT LOVE: PERSONAL STRUGGLES

||

FOREVER LOVE YOU: LOVE ON

||

Others will be coming as time goes on:

SO GO ONLINE AND IN THE SEARCH ENGINE ON **AMAZON**, TYPE IN ***Jonathan Dekle***

Visit also my website @ jonathandekle.com

Thank you, may love carry us on.

CONTENTS

[Knight]

Knight in Armor
My demons closet reopened,
And ten popping out.
Another thirty were thirsty and hungry trying
to kill me.
So a dance with the devil came on.
People were like,
"Kid, who are you trying to kid?
Dark scary you tell, but is it real?"
I awake and shake,
For it was real.
Demons came in trying to still a soul,
Rob a child.
So saddle on I do with a Knight in armor, God.
Next on my left,
Fire demon of pure fire breathing as my
company.
A light filled heavenly radius angel on my right
side as company trustfully.
Let me back up,
Flying above me is love.
A backup company of angels of unknown
numbers.
Leading the battle.
You won't believe me,
But listen to me.

Can you hear my inner thoughts?
Can you see radio singles?
Can you see the not seen?
Can you see who surrounds me?
Can you understand I don't battle with just
humans?
I do, but who will always win?
For I fight with demons of the highest levels that
any human I face is just a faze.
But I never skip their case,
For I wouldn't want them to skip mine.
I want to be friends,
Show love and compassion,
For as I fight,
I fight with love,
And love is my company.
Meaning you are my company,
My many of fellow brothers and sisters;
Young, old, in between, all green, yellow, blue,
black, white and golden brown.
All us love each other around.
Been taught from the wises of wises.
Look at my eyes,
Look into my soul.
What do you see?
See unknown beauty.
But understand what I see when I look out up
thoughtfully through such;
A power higher than any understands.
Gods power.

I don't always see,
But when I look up and believe,
I do,
For God is power.
Is All.
When I see the connections.
I see through the filter seeing a pure picture of
imperfections turning to pure perfectly
perfected perfections.
I see for God has opened my eyes to see.
Do you see?

[Awaken Shaken]

He awakes shaken for not awaken sooner.
Look out and see an oncoming storm.
Wonder why he still here anyway. Lives all on
his lonely.
Goes on humming maybe one day he wouldn't
be.
But look, y'all—
Maybe I'm crazy just as you.
Just as we all are.
We all wild young free and us.
Add us together and better be the outcome.
Look at each other, some shy, adorable, wild,
funny, hyper, inspired, motived, seekers,
improvers, teachers, learners, followers etc.
To tell us a part as individual beings.
Look at me—
I'm just a lover,

A brave soul of believing,
A Knight in armor,
An inspired individual with vivid details—
Knowing we all can achieve better.

"Ah, I know I'm a multilayered being who fights
devils and death."
How can he be such a being some ask?
I'm gifted as any,
I sought deep within to see the full me.
Saw it all and almost passed out—
For it was that fulfilling.
Seeing the good,
And the bad.
Filing something heavy,
Getting ready to find its clarity,
Opening that Bible,
Seeing the mapping connections to final true
realities to all things.

[Up]

I look up!
Wonder what's up?
Say maybe today things will be different,
Look out;
Seeing maybe not.
Come out, kicking, knocking down those locks;
those walls—
Saying maybe I can shock and do something
different.

Different being Lil Old Me.
Setting me free.
Opening up,
Praying dear God,
Let me be me free.
Living correctly,
Living to what is right.
But do so freely as me.
Not to what people think I should be.

[Runner]

Running as the runner.
Some say I'm only getting dumber.
But others say day to day I'm only getting funner.
Hunted as the hunted so running away from the hunters.
Elder utters usher in negativity.
Mothers fight back with positivity.
I set back and try to find myself settled.
Scream back all I'm trying to do is find sweetness in any bitterness cause I'm only after better-ness.
I witnessed hell for a tale of a blood tale of a bell that has been sung.
I do not run as a runner towards such devils.
I come and fight back at such with Holy Scripture hatchets.
My stomach stops when sin starts it hip-hopping for it's too much to have it happen.

I drop and pray for the Bible to come over run
my evilness.
I try and think me and God can come to an equal
platform but find myself,
So I lower myself before God to re-stand.
I once upon a time was a man who thought of
everything and anything and loved it.
Still I am so,
So don't think am not,
But I try not to think of negative thoughts for I
cannot commit such hazards things to my
emotional self.
I sought out to find what true good and evil was
and became a king of a demon of it.
Speed Demon Redeemer appeared and then
Prime Lion came roaring soaring exploring and
boring down any humanity left I had.
Did a couple spells saying that was true and the
next thing that happened made me come
slapping myself till I was partly mad and sad
from kidnapping myself.
A lad dropped down to such a low level that
devils were his accompany.
I was pushing to start my own blood killing
company for any.
By sharing evil,
Bringing others to my level of gone-ness.
For any is welcome to hell.
But also is any to heaven.
I now hate myself for such devilish crimes

committed.
Black magic was tragic for I wrote and wrote
and whatever I wrote came happening.
Some may say that is awesome,
But not if you understand at what price.
So now the true mapping is discovered, and now
true devils find true me and true me is true
power for I stand behind God.
But it would seem whatever I try to do happens.
Maybe I'm some special child or maybe time
happened and miracles happened.
But it doesn't matter either way I know hell is
all I deserve for what I have done.
And so much worst for what I still do some days
that I cannot allow myself to make it to those
heavenly gates,
For any and all heavenly above should hate
someone like me, for I am truly horrible.
But God I know forgives and says,
"Don't listen to that devil's voice.
Son your sins have been forgiven.
Come home.
Believe in Me.
Come to Me.
I Am the way,
The Light.
The Pathway.
I Am the I Am.
I Am Forever and Ever."
- God

[Me Free]

Let me be me free.
Living correctly,
Living to what is right.
What is right to the Bible.
But do so freely as me.
Not what people think I should be.
For it's not their place to judge.
Only Gods.
Me free.
Me, me & God.
— Sir Knight Writes—

[Come As]

I may come across as someone stronger than a
lion mountain.
But deep down I fight demons and devils daily.
It's why I pray to God daily,
Even if some days I hear nothing back.
I try my hardest to fight the demons back to
conquer evils falseness.
I walk alone mostly,
For nobody wants me.
Leaving to reflect back at myself always
wondering what I'm doing so wrong.
Settling saying maybe some days I act too
rashly.
Sadly it's human nature.
A side of me I hate.
But it's what I was served,

So I take a step forward to accomplish what I
know to be the right pathway, Knowing there's
always room for improvement.
Even if I am miles apart from a single soul,
It's okay;
For I am the perfect loner there can ever be.
For even if I don't talk to anybody,
I talk to demons and angels all the time.
Having a higher level of company.
Many won't ever be able to understand that.
But at least I do.
Some may call me crazy,
But who isn't if they are so differently put
together.
I could hide all of me,
And not live,
So that I would be seen as normal.
But then I wouldn't want to live another day,
For then I would be trapping myself away.
I was made to share who I am.
Made to be someone who takes the hate,
And turns it into love.
For I am that middle ground filter.
Filtering out the dirt and making it into gold.
God, Jesus and the Holy Spirit is my company.
Leaving, I walk with heaven next to me always.
Leaving nothing is impossible, rather simple if
you let God work through us all to bring Heaven
back to us sooner than later, will you accept
Jesus? For He loves you dearly.

[DEATH | GOD | US | FIGHT]

By and by die sides on inside.
All wishing I could die.
For why try?
Why try when you could simply die?
Yes, I sigh,
And say I'm only kidding.
Bidding death.
A stone could do my work.
A fly.
But why me?
Who am I?
I am nothing.
Death sounds so bitter sweat.
For then I could finally sleep.
Not having to think.
Not having to face such an evil race.
I bid all of it to myself,
Didn't I?
Death talks,
"You gave me your soul,
Remember?"
Yes of course,
I won't live a day not remembering.
But you never gave what you said.
So the strings fell apart.
My heart doesn't belong to you,
It never did.
So get that to your head.

Death why try me?
Why?
Am I so lovely to keep?
Do you long to have me?
For you know your nothing without me?
Do you weep? — creep, Death!
Weep!
You're only a faded away pasting age to decay.
Should I say your name death?
So you know—
Go run hide,
For you're only a pasting ride.
A dying tide.
On the wrong side.
You and I know misery,
For you created it into history.
How long must we play this player record of
recorded records?
We could play all day and all night and your still
be gone done away with history.
You beg me to love you?
But forget I do not love evil.
Forget I am a soaring eagle!
We mingled,
Created even sequels.
Qual to hell over and over.
But let me remind you who killed Jesus—
You!
Jesus forgave me, even you,

But you chose death.
Now you are death.
Yes, we walk and talk.
But we are not alike.
I walk with legions of heavenly Angels—
You walk with legions of demons.
We out number you two to one.
Yet you still try to reason with me and kill me.
Haven't you learned who controls?
Haven't you gone down through and through
earth roaming helplessly for more time?
Now your time has come.
You shall be king.
You shall be king over all of earth.
But remember,
You're death.
So you shall become death.
And fade away to never be again.
You chose this.
You wrote your own ending.
Let your demons gain full power.
Let them tower high and low.
Let them echo how unjust you are.
Their god.
Let them say aloud how God was right.
Let them hunt you down for a thousand years.
Fighting them with a death whisper.
For they will kill you over and over for what you
have done.
You will beg to die.

You will cry blood of tears as Jesus did.
For you will feel everyone's lost souls pain,
Hatred and misery.
All of what you created.
You will feel it all.
It will take a thousand years to feel for ever soul
you lead wrong.
This is your song you created Lucifer.
My friend, my dearest of so.
You chose this.
You just couldn't let your pride go.
Now go,
And do what you began.
Run for your time is almost out.
I loved you, almost called you a forever friend.
But in the end,
All you could do is think of yourself.
Creating your own prison den.
Sin.
Your demons even began to have remorse.
Trying to change their ways.
Maybe some will be saved,
This is not for me to say.
But I will say God is Just.
You all know this best of all.
He loves you even still to this day.
You were His creation.
Such perfection in all ways,
Until confusion came.
Until sin was created.

Until you became the fallen.
It broke His heart.
Tore it to pieces.
Why must you still follow your master of evil
demons?
Yes, you are bewitched to,
I understand.
But I will still fight for you,
For love conquers all.
So I must love you.
Even Satan,
But I will not follow and reflect his reflection of
pure disgrace.
It's why his face is gone.
Why he hides from you.
He's waiting for God to bestow his full angelic
powers back.
God has already been over the last century.
Just look how evil has taken over again.
Lucifer the morning light.
Shall be once again himself,
But with the self he created.
Glorious from the outside,
But death in the inside.
God promise him He would do so.
So it shall be done.
But remember you took the same cup as him.
Meaning death will be your end result.
For if you follow him,
You follow death.

I do not know all of the ages of earth as you.
But I do know you do.
Why not enlighten those you torment?
Why not set them free?
Why have to die more than twice over for being
responsible for bringing another to hell?
Why I cry!?
Why let yourself have to feel that?
Yes, they all tie back to satan.
The sins he shall pay for them all.
But why oh why pay for sins you could have
stopped?
Humans, me—
Why lead others away when you could be the
reason to why someone is saved?
Just show love.
Find love,
For God is love.
Yes, we do not have any saving powers.
We do not even have love.
But God does.
He will bestow you with grace, mercy, love, and
forever forgiveness.
You still have time.
Ask and it shall be yours.
Have remorse and change your ways.
Pray with all your hearts to be saved,
And you will.
Follow the Ten Commandments.
That's all that has to be done.

Repent and follow.
God is simple.
Satan is not.
Satan is a mockery, a false replica of God.
He sounds and acts as He.
But trust me, he is not.
He's so bent on killing that he will try and be God,
For he knows that's the only way to hurt God.
Don't be mislead,
Stay ahead looking up to heaven.
Jesus won't ever touch this earth again.
Not until the new earth is made.
So never follow a walking so called
'Jesus' for it won't be Jesus at all, but satan.
The seventh day is the Sabbath, it always have
been, and always will be forever and forever.
It's the only Ten Commandment that says
remember, God knowing we would forget.
Do not forget love.
For love sets us all free.

[Dark Valleys]

Though I walk through the valley of death,
I'll forever love on.
Though I talk with monsters,
I'll forever forgive.
Though life will show many colors,
My banner will forever show peace.
Though I don't know my next exit and entry,

I'll forever walk doing all I can do bettering all
and anything I touch.
For love lives on—
Lives on in song,
In our palms by us letting our love flow out
flowering its power.
Looking up praying dear God.
I'm just me.
Yet it leaves me wanting to express such words
the world will never be the same once I'm done.
For my passion will capture life,
Trapping them forever in words,
Leaving my actions to be expressed
automatically.
Leaving me to ask,
Who's riding with?

[Once Upon a Time]

Once upon a time I walked down a road.
I saw life,
Saw a knife right at my chest.
Me saying man,
"Sir Knight you can't make it.
Man that knife looking amazing."
Amazing grace.
Been singing it lately feeling heart heavy.
Saying man,
"You can do it."
Saying I'll post what I used to do so amazingly.

I'll write a rhyme level settlement.
A poetic rap.
I'll snap and slap a happy face on.
Once I was in a basement and chilled with a
brother that wasn't just a bother but an angel.
For heart being heart heavy,
Death ready,
He being happy and cheerful left me heart
ready for living on in this painful world.
Seeking for another breath knowing I can do it—
For if he can live on,
So can I can.
Years past on.
Me still hitting heart heavy,
Now looking seeing all I been through.
Saying man,
Let me shine love,
Let me be happy,
For my Grandma would want me to be.
My Mamma would want me to also.
Let me praise God,
Let me thank you all.
For even though I have little fiends,
I have love.
I have you all.
Even though some days I may see life is messed
up,
I'll look up to y'all,
And say—

Hey man thanks for being you,
Thank you for your smiles,
For your smiles make me smile and love.
How many souls I have seen and seen angels is
beyond words.
Thank you for your smiles.
Thank you for your love.
Thank you for you!

[All or Nothing]

As he opened his eyes he faded away into the
darkness of the day,
Disappearing into his shadows, pouring his soul
out before his days slowed.
Hoping as he fell his wings would grow so he
could show a show and tell of his life's forever
telling tale, throwing his love up into the air to
all, so if he fell and ended up in hell,
His love story would forever still tell his life's
forevermore love letter tale to any it fell upon.
Knowing,
God loved him,
So he never would end up in hell,
Even if he felt like that's all he was ever worthy
of.

[Love Deserved]

As he turned to mourn the outcome cast of
downward seen sin city.
He saw love risen in the air.
He wondered why they never understood it all.

He always wanted to gain such light from the
past,
But never has gotten it,
He always wanted love,
But never has gotten it yet.
So he sees life and love as it is—
A passing away day,
A day to choose which to hold onto;
Love or Hate?
Choosing love—
Loving it always,
But wishing it off everyday for someone desires
and deserves it,
But he,
Maybe never does, so he thinks,
But knows,
Those are his sad days,
That everybody deserves life.
Deserves love.
Even him.

[Filing Life]

While you find yourself more and more.
Remember to close each chapter of life
correctly, to help you move on.
But so ghost don't reappear from your closet.
Rather only surprises of loving gestures.
— Sir Knight Writes—

[Sorrows Talk]

Sorrows talk for tomorrow.
Narrow tunnels for the shooting mocking
arrows.
Grows the crowds of the ravens and crows.
Darkness falls, it calls, it hollows halls bawl.
Shouting y'all:
"Ye meek turn to weak now seek.
Flee evil or believe me when I speak."
Me hearing it's bellowing meowing,
Coming in telling its stories.
Humming its melody.
Hmmm shall die, umm we will hide,
At least we tried, maybe we shall fly, umm-te-
dumb numb thumb ups—
Oops, hiccups!
Me looks up—
Sorrow filled after drinking its cup of poison.
Seeing it's a prison.
Person within not knowing what's happening
without seeing clearly,
Having a third eye, yes not the one many know
of.
God spoke,
Saying look and see.........
Miracles of knowledge of foreshadow-ment
Seas of worlds experiments, testaments—
Basement hell doors entertaining entries
arenas—
Heaven opened its gates filled with joyous
wonderful wonders—

Of marvels of love, of happiness;
Forever healthiness—
Of God living directly by us.
See both sides clearer than the word hello.
Me in a hell-hole heaven hole all in one.
How oh me how is that true?
Do you not know who is beside me?
Maybe some do, but many won't ever.
I'm just like you, but mind inclined to higher
climbing levels, Jesus guiding, God directing.
Entered into a game and found it was reality.
Now I smile and act as nothing is happening.
But once in a blue moon, I must speak.
Or be swept away fallen down into the gray day.
Maybe mayday cries aloud—
All seeing eyes see and scared of what they see.
I see and scream—
Cry,
For I understand what's about to happen.
But do you?
You sow what you plant and get what you reap.
Now let's weep or stay asleep.
I'm just a messenger,
I'm still half way asleep.
So don't freak.
We still have time,
But maybe we don't.
This is not for me to say.
— Sir Knight Writes—
#LoveOnForeverInGodWeTrustAlone

[Dreamt of Past Days]

I view out and see life.
With it coming straight with a knife.
Without a true friend,
Not even a wife,
But oh how do I love life!
For I do me living high off life closing my eyes
and picturing olden golden pure days.
Minds bipolar as a blind polar bear in Hawaii
some days.
Cold crisp yet warm and out to say oh hi-ya
doing y'all?
Deep down depressed more than the saddest
soul alive—
So far gone nothing even feels as though I'm
alive yet.
So I shift through the emotions saying I know
them all so well—
It's a slide show of who I want to be sometimes,
And other times of who I never want to be.
Leaving me to say aww man,
How that even happen again?
I come in laughing and saying aww man—
Well....I went to bed one day and never woke up
So I think I'm still dreaming,
Or am I?
Alive eyes closed;
Soul open—
Heart open—

Knifes darted through my heart flooding blood
everywhere,
Yet still alive am I.
Why oh why doesn't one awake.
But wait,
I already awake marching on walking the fine
line in the mind of an Einstein—
Intertwined with a demon and angel as my
company with its demon head off walking off a
cliff thinking it's a mountain saying it's out for
the love fountain?
But wait for my heads already a blood fountain
turned into a love fountain—
Or is this just too crazy—?
Me living to much in past hells prison den?
So it must be a dream.
Dream on I do—
Dream on,
Rings on in the song.
The dreamer goes on dreaming;
Bringing on whatever reality once I awake.
For once I do,
I'll shake and bake like a lava crown coffin.
Walking talking as I always was,
How I always was supposed to be.
Just little to nothing by myself,
But opening my eyes awaking from my deep
begone nightmare—
Looking up to heaven,
Saying,

God is love.
So I am loved.
That, that was the past me,
Whose sins are covered by Love.
Amen.

[Excuse Me]

Excuse the me you haven't met yet.
Excuse the guy you used to think was so down
right me.
Excuse even me for not being fully me!
Excuse all of old me!
Welcome oh welcome,
Welcome the free minded opened enlighten
insightful delightful hyper active proactive
triple five star all in one soul—
The vibing thriving living loving giving serving
positive self me.
It's me; I won't hide all of me.
Only divide me into hundreds,
For me to be me,
My dearest me,
My me,
Wouldn't I be considered crazier than crazy?

[Life Coming at You]

Life will come at you.
Will test you.
Bet with you,
Saying man,
You can't even do a single thing.

You must jet out—
Fly out—
Come out and say na, no—!
But I can do it!
Bet I can't? —
Just watch.
Look at the little nobody gone out and say I'm
somebody,
But hide behind it all for by that time,
People will not even know a single thing to me
for they choose not to.
I walk alone begging not to be—
But I look out and say I have faith,
One day I won't be alone.
One day it'll be me and you,
Us together.
People be saying that's selfish;
I'll be like look on a bookshelf,
And you'll find me,
Over and over—
But you never cared to know me,
So I went under ground to a nobody who did
everything as everybody—But didn't take credit
for it,
For I was created into the ghost,
So the ghost I'll be.
The love ghost.
Lost to the air,
But shooting darts;
A million at a time.

Walking with angels pushing away devils saying;
Don't judge me.
They at least were my friends from day one.
At least they know me,
You don't,
At least not yet.
For that's too much for you to handle.
I battle myself daily.
On top of that,
Fight to survive to be accepted and in the end,
Come to say,
Screw it.
I'm me,
Period!
Say what you want,
My willingness to care just isn't there.
For I been hurt that much.
That I'll only care if it's to uplift someone else.
Then I'll care to the utmost.
For love is my motto;
Is my life—
God's love.
Lives on—!
— **Sir Knight Writes** —
[Spin]

The mind spins.
Thinking within what gives.
Quizzing the questions till answers are found.
Plundering under over under and be-yonder;

Longing for the sound to make sense.
Sending signals wide and far.
Signaling his love,
Wishing a fallen star wish with a kiss;
Leaving this a miss note until the arrival of her.
For my boat is afloat yet sinking;
For my heart notes play;
But our delayed.
Plays and continues, But the sound is saddened.
From the silence given.
So the mind spins on,
Receiving signals of life.
Messaging out the messages until then.

[Mapping Life]

We can go on forever in the middle of nowhere,
Exploring hiding away from the world,
Just doing life.
Can open new albums just cruising down a road
worrying about nothing.
Searching for new places that leave us wishing
we can stay there forever.
We can take a picture of life and see a movie
within the film.
For so much is happening.
Can walk straight into a million people just to
see the vibe we get—
Then ride along past.
We can be hidden in the tin can souls roaming

around loving it all.
Taking what we see interrupting it into
something forever memorable.
Out in the woods gone away from city light.
Having true starlight.
Laying—
Knowing all will be alright.
Can walk straight through a fight knowing love
be the end result. Peacing —
Vibing life like puzzle pieces.
Leaving new creations to be made always.
For settling for nothing regularly vibes on
inwardly.
Only fading away lost away,
Saying, please help me find my way back home
GPS,
But wait—
We're on our way to somewhere,
Viewing life's pages,
As we page through the ages writing down the
pages.
Marking our favorite places,
Dodging the bad ones.
Staying onwards homeward to heaven.
Finding the way as we walk on in the way we
know is right.

[Uncaged]

A day without music is like a day without you.
Not as lively,

As beautiful,
As thriving.
Life's driving gliding through the waves.
I'm just waving behaving saying all's amazing.
I'm doing me gliding off pure imagines of crazy
haha!
For I'm done trapping me,
The real me—
Doing me,
Smiling, laughing,
Not talking,
Then talking a lot.
Mirroring me,
Grabbing the steering wheel.
Being real,
Saying what's to hide?
I got too much to share.
A shareholder of love.
God's my Leader,
Me the seeker.
The befriender lover giver.
The gentleman.
Sad low,
Depressed second guessing everything once and
a while,
Hiding that.
Walking straight face ahead out of the cage,
Giving nobody any negative power over me.
For I did,
Done that,

My Mirrors Reflection

Too long ago.
Now playing a new song,
A love song.
Grabbing life's heart,
After already taking it a part,
Knowing every inch of it,
So I try—
Placing more down in the ink pages;
Some think,
Boy you're crazy.
Haha no,
Do you know me fully?
No,
So leave me be me.
Get to know me.
I love all,
But please don't try and go and judge me,
For I will only always try to help you.
But the second I'm judged,
It's hard for me to stay me and assist you.
For it's as though being trapped back into a
cage.
And I won't like that.
I'm free.
I'm me.
God only judges me.
Love me.
I love you.
#LoveOn

[Shaped to Be]

Shaped to Be
Many forget who I am.
Which is okay,
I never was meant to be so known.
I always was supposed to be the ghost of
yesterday which people saw;
Even thought they knew,
But never did.
I was meant to be the guy who walked into the
room,
And 'disappeared' scanning and thinking heavy
into everything,
Taking each word said,
And action that was done,
Cherishing it.
For everything seen was as though it was the
last time ever to see it.
So the cherishing memories behind it would go
straight to my heart.
I never was the bookworm guy who would read
and take it to heart, for if I did, it would have
ruined my being.
I had to find who I was first.
If I haven't—
School would have turned me into a genius of
destruction on my very own soul.
Creating me someone they wanted me to be,
Not who I would have naturally been.
No,

I wasn't made for any of that.
I was made the messenger.
The person who didn't have any real friends,
For only then could I say and walk away
knowing loneliness was already my steady
company.
So out of love,
I would say the things those who wouldn't want
to take the heat for, should have said.
Was shaped to be hated by all.
Made to be so broken,
My very soul could weep for centuries.
With such sadness comes such pity.
It's a pathway I was given and mastered.
Finalized to perfection.
The passionate genius of words.
The poet of life.
The messenger of God.
Messenger of love.
I love all I encounter.
Yes,
I am still human,
So such perfection of love is still in the works.
But look in my eyes,
And listen when I say something—
Do you hear the passion?
The love?
The care?
The self of me talk that has walked countless
miles?

Such a gift of emotions into words was always
me.
Mind playing with words for years, never
knowing the why to the reasons.
Thrown into a rap level of a game that tore my
very being apart,
Made me some mad monster,
For I had to be so that I would understand all
levels of everyone.
Even what to kill was like,
For words can kill a million times over.
Even knew what lying was,
Mastered it till perfection.
Knew all evil so I would know how to see the
truth.
Yes,
Jesus took such evilness and made it into love.
By giving me His love.
For it was always His plan.
Gave me a face that was so inviting,
That those who didn't know me would come
close so that I could show love,
show what real life is all about.
So who am I?
I'm simply me, I always have been.
Telling you to be you, for there's no need to be
someone else but yourself.

[Mind Jump]

If someone could jump into my mind for a
second,

They would feel as though they gained all real
valuable wisdom.
At first they would completely love it.
Until they realized the pain that comes in
having such a blessing.
They would learn that with such responsibilities
comes great heartache.
For to truly understand and feel everything and
be connected too, leaves realness to everything.
Leaving to, some days not wanting to get into
anything at all.
For the second put into play,
The passion and drive to understand goes from
zero to a hundred trillionth of a second,
Turbo mind spinning thinking to solve in
seconds.
Why be compared as a computer?
That comparison to a computer has always
seem right.
A computer has always been designed to sync
with the human mind in a way it can relate and
correspond to you,
So it feels natural.
Have you ever noticed how those who seek to
still keep learning can always figure out a
computer faster than those who seek to just be
given the how to?
Leaving people scared to hear such truth
sometimes.
Leaving me somedays not wishing to speak

anything.
For the answers are in the messages.
If I choose I could crush and tear you apart just
as fast as I could help and lift you up so high
that you would feel high off the idea of life.
See: being human we have two choices.
To be an evil knight of earth or a serving Knight
for God and help others.
I choose to work for God,
But even in that,
Some days my sinful self steps in;
My immature still growing side shows,
discrediting who I'm still trying to become,
But don't you understand to truly grow and
learn, messing up is the best way even if
heartache is usually the outcome.
I'm thankful for being foolish while young and
wiser now as I grow on.
I have so many questions that only God can
answer that it leaves me baffled, confused.
For why make me so able to connect things?
But so limited to connect everything somedays?
I understand it's Your time, not mine.
But why let someone feel more pain in their life
than happiness?
How can that be Jesus's love?
How is that love?
Am I suppose to go through so much worse than
this,
That this will be confirmed as love right now

with life being so simple?
If that's the case,
Even still more love could be given.
I know I talk out of frustration,
That love has been given and given again.
Leaving me playing cold chicken until I know.
For why roll a boat to an unknown location?
Even if you know the home location is heaven;
That still leaves me on a human level wanting to
know more.
It's who we are.
You know this.
So why block Yourself from me?
Am I truly that far gone?
Or is it that my faith is so weak,
That you seek for me to simply just trust more.
If so,
Why should I even try to better another day
knowing I'm only a fallen being?
Tell me that so that I can know.
All I know more than anything else is pain.
Which pain causes more pain until your
completely heartbroken.
But that is me still holding on to anything right,
As in seeing the pain and trying to never let
anyone else feel such as I have.
The second I would say no more to bettering,
that feeling would fade, but so would I and then I
would surely die, but the pain would turn to
complete hatred.

Why allow such a thought to even come across
my mind?
We all are special,
Able to achieve anything possible if You allow.
So allow faith in and understanding to come,
So confusion can't develop,
Rather fresh beautiful clarity.

[Your Light]

Life's a funny thing.
You can do one thing and have another million
things appear from just that one thing.
I speak and the power behind can shake the
grounds.
See what just happened there?
See it was multi touch,
Multi-meaning,
Multipurpose servings for it was such a broad
statement given.
Meaning it could hit anyone in a million
different little ways,
As many ways as they can directly relate.
I could hate,
Devastate and do a retake on my past done
actions and gain a new passion from such if I
choose.
Or I could take and take any hate and turn into
pure love from above,
Giving actions of passions that leaves
mountains falling or growing.
Many never cared to know me, actually me.

I am to blame,
But at the end of the day,
I'm in a bigger game than anyone in fame or
ever named living could ever understand
besides my name,
For it's my life,
My Journey,
My time to do me.
How could I come out and say such a thing?
Face demons and devils and high offices then
you would understand.
When you can't even count on one hand a true
friend,
Besides 3 demons and 3 others,
Being Jesus, God and the Holy Spirit.
Then you will begin to understand the ring I
stand in.
Next to the highest to the lowest.
And somehow I got lucky to be placed right in
the middle.
Middle in my family and in the middle of the
largest thing earth will ever have to happen.
Leaving me to say this:
For it's time to begin the end.
Once things spend and start to come to an end;
Who will you give your all too?
Some days I fall.
Somedays I call and hear nothing.
Understanding all I ever wanted was love but
never received it in a real enough way to call

mine.
Only spiritual beings could give such.
No human could ever withstand such as me—
Perhaps some could, but I have yet to meet their
precious real living motto genuine souls.
Many can never relate fully to me, which is ok,
Or at least not opened enough to admit such.
Many can't understand just who I am.
I either until it all came crashing together
letting me know clearly who I am.
Leaving my hands shaking.
I'm a leader.
A teacher.
A mentor of love.
A follower of God.
Never again a follower of evil.
Cause I won't ever be that person of bad ever
again.
If I do,
I'll kill myself first.
For I won't go against love.
For love is all I ever wanted.
So love is all I'll ever give and be.
For who I am,
Really?
I'm just as you,
Different in my own ways,
As you are in yours.
Me just reflecting on myself on a high note,
So nothing can be missed,

But truly at the end of the day,
I'm no different than you.
All I am is a person shining his light.
Battling the same battles as you.
Sharing my reflection because I care,
Care for you.
— **Sir Knight Writes**—

[Face Off]

Even though I may face demons of unknown
amounts,
I must put my head high,
And say if they try to kill me so hard,
I must be something they are fearful of.
If God doesn't reveal Himself to me,
I know enough of Him to keep living.
Even if I must go through fires hotter than lava,
I'll still stay head high trying to give all a piece
of peace.
Yes days will come where my immature self will
come and show more than my loving self,
And when those days come it will discredit me,
But see that's the problem you can't look at me
and see me as someone perfect, or even good, if
you do, all you will see is someone broken apart
to million of pieces tryin' to put myself together.
Someone out hunting for survival, someone who
rides Live Free or Die Hard Trying to Give Peace
to All as my living motto.
That side of me was hidden,
But I won't hide it any longer.

Even if I must walk the loneliness road
imaginable,
I will still stay head high.
Even if demons must be my company,
I won't cave in.
I don't seek anyone anymore,
For the road of such will always bring me down,
For how could I want such,
If they won't be such.
I don't cry for myself,
I don't lie either.
I just will be real.
I gave people more opportunities than possible
to seek after me.
Now that side of me will forever be hidden.
Hidden in books, videos, & actions...
For I will not preach to a wall any longer.
I will not reflect such perfectness if I cannot live
it fully myself,
I will be the shadow.
The hidden man who has such light,
That I will not be hidden at all.
But I won't be showing me.
I will be trying to show God.
When someone looks at me,
They will see what they see.
I will enact actions by words.
Not by real done actions always.
For until I am perfect,
It is not my place to show such a light.

I can only try.
For I judge myself so high,
That God Himself has hidden from me,
From me being so downright fallen.
I do not blame Him at all, for I can't.
All I have ever been is the perfect median.
Never even a true normal human being.
So it feels every single day.
For if I have been,
I wouldn't be here saying such,
I would have an actual life,
That is seen as 'normal'.
I'm trapped in a hell hole of my own creation.
Played with the devil and what do you expect,
Except walking next to his highest levels of
demons daily trying to kill me.
Since I have fallen so far down,
I will forever have to live with its company.
I will not be able to reason with,
For nobody can reach my level of understanding
on this subject unless they too used to follow the
devil fully as I did.
If I'm lucky once I say this,
I will be dropped from such a high calling.
I tell God, I never was meant for any of this,
For if I were,
Then why would I be saying such words?
Do they truly help others?
I feel like all I talk about is myself,
It is my reflection book,

So it's acceptable,
But do I say to much?
Why would heaven be pouring tears over me?
Over us?
The fallen.
Why wouldn't God just show Himself?
Tell me something.
Why let demons walk with me more than
angels?
All I ever wanted was true love,
Why was that too hard to give?
Why was that too much to ask?
Is it i'm just not ready for such?
I know love, but know nothing at all about it.
I am so damaged by love,
That I can't even tell people I love them
sometimes.
I can't say I even do in that moment,
They are just another person to me,
Someone as the rest.
Once I understand this mindset,
I snap and ask God for the positive mind set—
Where I see people,
And only love.
For my eyes of compassion are opened.
My self is refreshed and renewed.
Rebooted to start over again.
For once we think we hit the end,
We truly have only reached a new beginning.
— **Sir Knight Writes**—

[Dark Days]

Even if dark days come,
I will not let go of the love from above.
I will forever give all my heart to God even if
somedays the blindness in doing so is unknown.
I know my faith is weak,
But my courage to walk on,
To move on—
To better loving all—
Showing it—
It drives me on strong.
Ties me to the will to want to do so.
My flesh is weak,
But my seeking to perfection is so high that
even if I fall a billion times the will to keep
moving forever on leads me on!
That the life I have been given has so much
potential when God becomes a part of it,
So much insightful wisdom to share.
How could I be so blessed?
How could I be so strong?
How could I be so stubborn that it makes me
stupid some days?
How could I be so different?
So ever connected that I can touch anyone's
heart?
Is it that it is my gift to everyone—
Is to share such passion with such convention
that it moves anyone, moves mountains.

Somedays I wonder how much is me, and how
much is You?
For even if my mind and my actions can detour
off course,
You know my heart and read my heart.
The patients You have is beyond understanding.
The love You give is so freely,
So irreplaceable,
So connected.
You all are so special,
So irreplaceable to God,
That know you are loved.
He has a place for you,
Forever in His Kingdom,
With forever serving services of work that
doesn't seem like work at all,
For it's so much fun, so much contentment and
purpose it's what life is all about.
Even if now sorrow and pain hurt you,
Follows you perhaps,
Know how we live in such a sinful world that it's
Gods way of preparing you for what's to come.
Life's filled with confusion,
With sickness, greed, pride, selfishness, and
painful heart-aching disaster.
But with Gods utmost love, they are those great,
wonderful blessings that are forever
empowering to the soul.
Are a forever reminder of love.
God knows all, just trust His ways.

And watch the blessings He gives.
If hard times come your way,
It's His way of readying you up for what's to come.

[Runner]

I run as the runner running for justices.
Seeing just how precious it truly is holding its treasures closely in heart and mind.
Sweet pleasures in steadiness,
Seeing maybe they have no meaning anymore,
For in the end it's only fading away to a fallen day, but see life is layers, all adding up, and up.
Some may say,
"Hey man, what you saying."
I'm like,
"I'm saying what and who I always was.
You just hearing it now."
Look at me,
I will say it.
Look at me,
You don't even know me.
Don't you dare act as you do.
Come step into my shoes.
Get my God enlightening insightful life views.
See behind this precious face is a forever turning racing changing mind who has so many painful, loving deep in-depth-full sides,
So I'm still growing to find myself—
I forever will be surprising.

Someone not lazy, not crazy,
But steady ready to tell you something that
leaves you wondering deeper into life's pages.
For you will never be ready to hear what I have
to say, for I am the messenger.....
So I'll just say it.
For if I say it now,
Imagine what type of seeds can be planet?
I'm the perfect person to tell you so much,
You believe you know me,
For I put genuine care behind talking to
someone, for come talk to me, & I'll love you.
But little to know you never will know me all,
For it's not your place to know me fully.
How can you know me, if I don't fully know me?
How can anyone say they know someone,
If the someone has never known themselves?
I can't ever reach out and onto others to bring
them to my understanding, at least not easily,
I have traveled so many years to get to where I
am, it's why I have pages of me written down.
I can only help those below my level of
understanding,
For to understand,
You must have experienced it somehow to be
able to make it have any value to you and to
others in a sensible way.
You can sense the realness and genuineness to
it all, seeing it all had to happen anyways.
I can try my best to help guide you on,

But I forever will sing my own song.
Having a song in Gods love.
Growing, attaching my song to yours.
But, I'll forever will be myself always.
Dodging demons and devils.
Flying with God and Angels.
Saying it's me in these pages paging through the
ages, somedays wishing I didn't have too.
But been honored and blessed to be allowed to
be the traveler through past times to present
and future.
Understand no one will fully understand that,
But those like me;
But as time goes on,
Tell me I am wrong,
And I'll take back whatever I said.
Leaving me faded away and off course compare
to the rest, till you understand fully.
For I do not get any rest still chilling here in
this time zone.
I look back and see time has only repeated itself.
Leaving me asking why must we still be doing
this to ourselves?
Saying anyone could predict the future,
It's so plainly evident to see.
Leaving me seeing such complexities as a
natural wake up call,
Saying, "Hello".
Wondering how I could really be the only one
seeing it.

Feeling maybe I'm someone made to glide over
everything,
So I can give an input advice that will always
leave you enlighten some how, some way.
Can't say how I ended up this way,
But at the end of day, it is that way.
Simply leaving me praying asking God why me?
Some saying man,
You so full of yourself and my response is:
Are you me?
No, so take what I say and say it's garbage,
Say what you want to say,
But it will bring out its truth more and more,
And once it does,
Then will you believe me,
But by then,
I'll be so far gone for I travel where I'm needed,
That you will be wishing only if I knew,
And I'll be saying kindly,
Well, now you do.
I give you all views of life,
For as the Knight in Armor,
I had to go through all to understand all.
Leaving I'm still very young,
I still have a lot of traveling and puzzling left to
do till Jesus comes again.
How about you?
We can teach each other life.
By sharing what matters to us.
— **Sir Knight Writes**—

[Steps]

Life isn't for the weak.
It's for those who seek to fight onto something
better.
Those who will never take a no for an answer,
But will fight for a yes,
For a no means they are giving up,
And the realist strongest will never allow that.
You must find passion in life.
Find that reason to breathe again and never let
that go in your life.
For if you do open that door,
To let go;
You are only opening a new door to a door way
downward that gets only darker and daker.
God comes in and takes you those baby steps,
For He prays for us all.
To help us lean onward up.
Those who are weak He will come in and help
make stronger.
So everyone can be kings and queens.
Uplifting wisdom is a power that can help us
make it through anything imaginable.
That we will never be done with life.
That life will only keep opening new pages and
new books.
Some write out a few pages in life.
Others write so many that they must release
those pages out to help others,

So they can fulfill their pages too.
I'm a leader,
A seeker for justice and peace.
Who are you?

[Straight Line]

I have learned,
To walk the straight line,
No one will appreciate you.
That if death would come knocking,
A part of me would run calling begging to take
me away from this painful world of sin.
For then what I say,
Would be taken to awaken.
Until then only the smart, teachable,
Will be the reachable ones.
For they seek to know knowledge and wisdom.
It pains me,
Beyond emotions to express.
History repeating itself.
That the truest form of love could be attained,
But is being rejected.
Leaving many days to question why should I
face another league of devils?
Tearing at my very soul,
Trying their hardest to rip it to pieces.
Whispering lies everyday at my inner soul.
Me walking on smiling acting like I'm just like
everyone else :)
Telling nothing about the higher level attacks.

For many wouldn't even understand a single bit
of it unless they too are spiritual.
Leaving me the loneliness soul.
For where ever I walk,
Battles of countless demons and Angels fight on.
Me feeling the battles always.
Leaving me to question:
Why me?
What makes me so valuable?
All I am is dirt and nothing more.
I talk to God daily,
Get little answers somedays.
For the answers I already received leaves me
grieving beyond words to express.
Leaves me wanting to walk straight into hell
gates to say, well now.....
Am I really that special as some filled demon
being again?
God coming in,
Pushing away such thoughts,
Showing love.
Leaving me wondering why,
Why am I being pushed so hard?
For God wants me to commit treason?
Swear it must be so,
Or why would I feel this way?
So special I can't be told nothing.
So special I must live by myself.
So special that hell lives in my soul some days.
For the loneliness kills over and over.

So special I could send this out and have people
panicking saying,
"It's all okay.
Things will get better"
Inner supportive self replying,
"One day,
One day it will be okay, promise."
But it's hard to live like this.
With monsters inside your head.
Leaving me to hold onto my Bible just that much
more pushing the demons away even further.
So my pathway can be guided on with light.
Gods heavenly filled lighted pathway.

[Faces]

Been dragged down low,
Been many miles rougher than this before.
Know the games played the second they are
being played.
Wish we didn't have to play this all over again.
Look over saying why you loving playing
messing with everyone, especially me?
As though you didn't know what was happening.
Saying I never knew,
Just only thought.
Whenever did my thinking always be so right?
Was it when I started to go down the right
pathway and started saying goodbye to the old
me lost wasted me.
The old rugged down drugged out me?

The second God came and said I forgive you,
Just simply follow Me.
Starting to guide me on homeward, having me
doing my homework.
Working on getting rid of the old me.
The stubborn selfish low dirty gritty pretty boy
toy story.
Washing away the day of him.
Smashing away the ray of him,
For its only an evil desire coming out of him,
Saying I'm creating a new desire wanting wire.
Inspired to saddle a new climbing ladder
upward to heaven.
Counting seven seven be my number.
Saying I'm counting onward to something.
Knowing one day,
I'll reach a new number never heard of before.
Exploring life.
Peddle to the metal type of vibe.
For it's a ride of a lifetime type of tide.
It's coming rushing pushing brushing an
interview.
I been interviewed by angels,
And devils for years,
How much realer can it get?
An interview with my Maker.
Making me shake,
Because I can't say I'm ready.
Leaving me asking why am not? Finding I know
why,

Leaving me wondering why my legs aren't
moving.
Changing, begging again for forgiveness.
Swear I'm two-faced.
Madden by a hidden face.
Knowing it's only a temporary reality.
For no demon nor devil can touch me.
Unless God says so.

[Spinning Dreams]

Waking up,
Saying dear God.
Another blank empty night.
Laying by myself,
Thinking by myself,
Wonder if all I have is myself?
Saying no,
There must be another like me.
Spring back in;
In the background.
Thinking a million questions.
Placing down the suggestions.
Pacing with its life filled emotions.
Wondering if my emotions are trustable.
Filled with pain by memorable encounters for
they are no longer here,
Leaving me here missing them dearly.
Fear of dust road endings unless You're here by
me and my family.
See sunset endings pretending there's no ending

cause You're always here.
Knowing there's no true ending,
But the feelings to such,
Can come in heavy.
Flooding my mind with despair.
Wishing I could just go and disappear.
Looking up hearing Your voice,
Whispering,
"Soon, and very soon,
I shall come!"

[Direction]

Running towards something better.
Thinking maybe I'll be someone better.
Thinking for a moment and wonder it.
Saying why does life have to send me this
direction and that direction.
Correcting myself asking why I keep heading
out of map quest requested suggestions.
Come to intersections with multiple outcomes as
its realities.
Genuine, special, filled with ideas to unknown
places.
Only got one body,
One life,
So which pathways do I start now,
And ones I start in 15 years?
Love history—
Keep looking—
Paving a way to something amazing.

Looking in magazines and seeing I don't want
these type of things.
Just wanting real things.
Feeling it's getting real here.
I'm talking emotional supportive things,
Things that truly matter in the end.
Seeing if I can be happy off simply no things,
Just imagine how happy I'll be once I got some
things, like friends and a family of my own.
Fixing course to beneficial things, Mazing out
towards better things, Keying in the coding to
Kingship
Leadership,
Printing in,
"Fix it, fix it, fix it!"—
Cause everything has gotten real sick here.
Sit befuddled with this puddle of water I see.
It' mucky,
Runny with overly optimistic views, yet still
sick to see its lucky reality showcasing still off
racing chancing its fortunes.
Mourning its scoring,
Horning its own warnings,
Pouring in its stormy puddles.
Rushing in now, or never.
Running towards something better, and trip on
the hellish scum.
Wonder who's dumb or just numbed?
Number one rule:
Following the Ten Commandments before the all

all the suppose to be 'fun'.
For the fun sometimes leads towards the gun.
Say I'll never be done till God says completion.
Me just living another day running towards
something better always.
Taking each day as a baby step.
Stepping up that Jacobs ladder.
Calling in the latter rain.
Praying we're all ready for it's getting heavy
with its fist ready, steady.
We're just lucky with us having still grace
covering us all.
God's amazing grace.

[Third Eye]

One eye open,
Then two.
They talk,
So you know....
Their connection going deep;
Almost getting into a third.
Gathering information.
Transmitting its data into a channel—
Compacting its connections into an unseen
unknown zone.
Leaving few to see.
But to those who do,
They are never the same again for the
information is its own eye.
Gods insightful enlightening eye.

His Holy Spirt.
Guiding, talking, directing.
Helping to map out the real things and the false
things. Seeing He guides us in more ways than
we will ever realize, for the third eye is Gods
own eye if you truly follow Jesus as your Lord
and Savior. There is also another third eye, a
false eye, that is of devil, it follows falseness and
false light, and it's power will never touch God's
power. It will show it's power one day, but God's
power will always over power it's power, just as
Moses rod over power the Egyptian's 'power' so
shall those who follow Jesus over power the
devils false light of power.
Believe in God fully and you shall be given this
Third Eye.
Open your eyes to heaven and see it's beauty,
Gods beauty and you shall indeed never be the
same again.

[Over Thinking]

See what I wanna see some days.
Feel it's in the air most days lately.
Come in heavy with a mind thinking crazily.
Why I say the same things over and over,
I don't know why goes on in the mind.
Walk in with bubble bundle full loads of different
pathway roads to float on.
Wonder if I can honestly ever walk on.
Know though I will,
And can,

So stand as a man I go, standing next to God.
Throwing thumbs ups to those still falling
calling out for help who are lost and confused.
Saying will situations ever change themselves?
I think not,
Unless we make changes ourselves.
Fixating towards bettering.
Tethering,
Gathering different things.
Challenging educational topics.
Tropical within feelings,
Giving those warm awesome loving times.
For enlightening sends down lightening to one's
very soul and heart.
Digging deeper into the fine lines—writing in
new files each day.
Unzipping a tripping flipping umbrella into the
sofa with a soda in hand smiling.
Asking which happened to this tasting with it
trapping? Get away devil!
Napping,
Snapping at life for slacking.
Ask me again what is life,
And I'll give ya one.
Run as a loner mostly,
Making me feel ghostly.
Go to my bed get into a ball and then it feels like
home again, nice and warm and peaceful.
Someone tries to summon me and I'm like
someone actually talking to me? No way,

Who would of guest?
Feel heart pain in the chest once I think about
it, that nobody ever wants me, only when it
benefits them do they want me.
Crazy after something that's not yet seen,
Maybe that's absurd, word—
Pure nerd which verbal adjective word you
saying? I'm just saying I'm missing you,
Yet forget why,
For it's all becoming blurred and numbed.
For I don't want to think anymore today.
Goodnight.
— **Sir Knight Writes**—

[Started Life]

Once started,
How you going to stop me?
You think of me as someone funny.
Honey, baby, who you thinking about?
Maybe not me, cause it's getting awfully
lonesome here.
Me knee in deep with life.
Lights heading on,
Turning on.
I'm walking on,
Loving it all.
Focusing on better things.
Traveling around discovering remarkable
progress leaving clear pictures.
Pictures of new days to come.

Seeing as we age we keep going through stages.
Paving these stages into pages.
Each stage starting us off onto something more.
Seeing the more changes towards bettering only
keeps life going on forward if we keep at it.
Knowing life has only just begun.
That Jesus has so much more for us awaiting in
Heaven, so stay course to bring Him back sooner
than later, messaging out, we are on target....
Keep sharing love and God....keep sharing how
God lives in you...that's all we got to do.

[Ashamed Game Played]

Ashamed I played a game.
Been looked on 24/7.
Cause I want heaven.
Seven seven be the day.
But maybe six six be your day.
Who needs satan suits if you can have Gods?
Why have and make foolish gods?
Why die for something you clearly been brained
washed for, understand real reality more.
Why kill to publicly prove to heaven your sick
point, why be so prideful you won't admit Gods
way is the best way there is?
Why point at me and say I'm the issue?
Why make your issues be blamed out on others.
Why not be a man.
Why not stand and kill your own devil inter self
devils?
If you don't,

You will die either way.
But if you bring millions with,
You will die,
Then die again and then the last time you die
will be forever to never be again—
Will feel so much pain,
That insane won't even be enough to explain
such evil game planned, played.
Y'all devils are lame,
Lamer than lame.
Be satan's clone.
Be his and he will kill you and not even care, but
laugh over it all.
He will try then to be God, aka satan will try;
But no angel above or fallen can dare come close
to His level aka God of the Most High level of
Glory.
The devil tricks.
It is why you have this passion to kill me
demons.
But save it,
You kill me,
You're only doing me a huge favor.
So I'll pray for y'all,
And hope you can save yourself by God the
Father and Holy Spirt and Jesus Christ grace.
Bring on your little-cloned pope.
I hope you aren't disappointed when God kills
him, for he is you and him is me to you.
Meaning we all people and are all the same.

Sinners. No one can ever stand in the place of
God for representation; only Jesus can.
Jesus lives in Heaven and the next time you see
Jesus will be the day He comes to take us home
in the clouds of heavens where all eyes can see
Him and His forever glory.
No game you play will ever make you a greater
human man, we all are sinners, which is okay, it
is why Jesus had to come and die for us all.
You can become demonized and after a while
and realize your still absolutely nothing,
But slaves heading to your abyss graves.
God only wants to save, but He will kill out of
love, for no evil can ever be again after He
comes again.
So kingdoms of Earth,
You have been warned and warned and warned.
The 3 angel's messages has been sent and sent
and is being told.
Carry out the devils planned plan since he and
his demons have been cast out of heaven and
invite death to your own souls.
Why fall?
Why brothers and sisters fall?
Why try to achieve the hall of fame to in the end
receive the flames?
Why play satan's game?
Why cast self down with him?
Why not look to Him Him who made you?
God.

Made us all,
Please listen, please.
Why contain brain dead maintenance with demons?
I know I sure won't.

[Nine & Three]

Life's turning,
Foreshadowing enacting reality.
Many tumbling in circles circulating similar situations all around us.
Each separating by direct mindset emotions seeing life all differently.
It's funny to say how we are all so far apart,
Yet so close together by us being humans.
Leaving the chance for opinions to plant new ideas everywhere if we allow.
Leaving life turning,
Foreshadowing its future by us breathing its opinions.
Plants of poison and plants of salvation.
Giving us a planet of damaged goods.
Circulating good and evil leaving us choosing who's turning where?
I got my steering wheel;
You got yours?
Which road channel tunnel do you challenge?
I know which one is right.
Do you?
I'm going right,

Who's got my 9 & 3?
I know God has my 6 & 12.

[Beautiful Life]

Waking up,
Seeing life as it is.
Something overwhelmingly beautiful.
Seeing out unto others,
Trying to make the world a better place.
Chasing after something special.
Feeling the love in the air.
Loving the feeling of living.
Giving as much as I can, to help everyone
understand what it is to live again.
Spent so many miles on windy wild roads to
send anyone a little crazy and dizzy.
Wonder if I left today would anyone miss me?
Looking closely at the fine print, wondering
what's next to put in the dint?
Getting onto some thinking be the next hint.
Forgetting any stopping block, unlocking stage
three rocking launching off towards heaven.
Knowing once launched, things will forever
change, for the end is nearer than near.
Stepping up to the stage, about to turn the page,
Looking into the mainstream waves seeing still
clear open oceans, for God controls it all.
Seeing inspiration from creation, seeing what's
in demand, and which sandbars to miss.
Leaning on sidelines,

Seeing each fine line,
Knowing which fishing line to call mine.
Gliding on God.
Riding on,
Scoping out what's next.
Finding life's complex if you get things to mixed.
Separated departmental selections of files to
life's full true meaning,
Leaving a clearer mindset.
Want my fishing net so full it's overflowing in
with new creativity.
Search engine beginning to ending.
Forever searching looking on how I could affect
the next in a better way with love in mind.
For the next may just see it even deeper.
Making me waking up seeing life as it really is.
Something absolutely completely beautiful if
you let it be.

[Maturity]

Once you begin to see how all these 'adults' for
years seemed so mature and smart to you:
Only because you weren't.
You now see since time took its place. You see
how immature and shallow society truly is,
Notice how huge of a problem that really
becomes in the larger scale of reality.
Leaving you fully seeing how misinformed,
naive, self-desiring, prideful,
And broken apart we are.
Separating us worlds apart,

Yet deep down keeping us all connected to the
idea of survival.

The question is:

What type of world do you want to work and try
and live in?

Keep pushing to make Earth are forever home,
or push open the gates to Heaven by us
preparing everyone for the final message.

Solutions: never stop learning.

Always be the bigger person.

Keep your word.

Have an open mind.

Follow moral rules of codes.

Think reason, logic and is it overall right before
letting emotions step in.

Keep visioning and dreaming.

Keep helping those who literary physically can't
help themselves in all ways possible.

Practice workmen-ship in all areas from a
young age till our death beds.

Have hobbies so you're busy,

Thus overall more content and happy, for life is
filled with meaning all around then.

Read more informative information than
useless,

Like read your Bible.

Balance your life finically, mentally, spiritually
and physically.

Don't let life stop you from having fun.

Be mature and responsible.

Know right from wrong,
So you only know how to show kindness,
Thus love.
Be adventurist.
Befriend all.
Listen to different opinions fully before speaking
so everyone is understood and appreciated.
Don't forget the past, nor future,
And make the present as best as possible.
Knowing our true home is Heaven.
Remember that supremely.

[Tasking]

Ever sit back and have to try to relax?
Being at each turning point thought to be an ax,
Mixed with,
"Hey son, relax, take it easy."
Five days later you tell yourself you took it easy,
Listened to yourself and see what you have to
show for it?
Did nothing and didn't accomplish nothing
worthy of calling accomplished!
Try to fixate it and fix it by eating some goals.
Having my morning oatmeal happy feel me up
with worthiness goal—
God feed me up happy goals-worthiness meal.
Placing me into a whole new reality.
Multitasking supporting each engines task.
Asking until finding which question mask face
has its place in this earthly fight sides of a race.

Shoe laces laced and ready to go race race!
Facing each racer as a friend.
Trying to blend in as needed but sending an
outgoing befriend pin to all.
Winning at one thing and that's living.
Sinning here and there, eyes opening, repenting
Knowing I can try and do better—pretending
nothing.
Living in the realness of it all.
Fear little, but enough to stay alive.
Seeing the only person to fear is God.
Trying to always improve and be even better.
Knowing God forgives and leads.
So each tasking morning,
I call to God,
So I can race on safely in this life.

[Gifted]

If you're gifted with the power that many would
die for,
How you suppose to handle that?
When you're in the middle of a fire and both
sides are trying to pull you apart,
What amount of stress would you have?
With a forever spinning mind,
Many not even able to fully understand
It's hard for someone to relate to me,
I swear......
Leaves me just trying to fit in, but the more I try
The more I depart off to my own walk.

Trying to figure it all out,
Write so much,
That it's a drug of its own.
More days than most I feel alone, trying to
connect to people,
And it turns awkward.
So I hide most of me and show and tell bits
because it seems to fit.
Locked in a prison.
Go through more changes than most that I
wonder if I have more than one face?
Seeing I wear many hats.
Glance in the mirror and wonder if my past still
lives on in me,
And if I die would I even live again?

Friends?
What friends seems to go off in my mind daily.
Know so many people,
But do I really know?
Focus on self to much,
I know,
But I live with myself,
And myself is the only true friend I have that I
know will keep me walking straight,
What about Jesus?
I talk and walk with Him daily.
Some days making Him cry rivers of blood,
I know, I admit I'm a sinner,
A sick minded devil.

Did so many things that I swear the devils in my
blood.
So connected to demons that I wonder if I'm
even fit to stay moving on forward to try to even
better—repent daily,
Over and over,
Yet still fading, falling calling out I can do
better?
Just if I would try too,
I know I could.
Wonder why my souls worth so much, wish I
could see the future better and clearer.
I'm told so many things that it's hard some days
to know who's telling me what.
Filtering its words out—
Digging deeper into it and finding myself
trapped even more by doing so.
For once I know, I know.
Sometimes freeing myself from stress,
And life by figuring the true reality,
Other times finding it's a curse to fully know,
But what you going to do.
Live half blinded or cry out and search for
answers until they are found?

[Once Upon]

Once upon a time the world was seen by me so
surprising,
Now so little does.
The opening new doors excited me, fill me with
wild child kid curiosity, made me question

where my footprint fell.
So many years went on....
Been to hell and back and now I walk many
more miles with scars.
Broken heart scattered with shattered broken
pieces of undone completions,
Wondering if failure is allowed to enter,
But deep down soul marathon runner winner of
something better keeps telling me,
No way, only success nothing less!
Once upon a time,
My mind and heart came together and made a
blueprint and mixed it with passion and vision.
Walking with a Bible and Angels managing.
God directing, trafficking, allowing me to keep
moving forward.
Wondering why me?
How many more once upon times, times does
my time allow me to have?
Seeing time as something precious, but knowing
it's not my time to really have.
Honored for another day of awakening.
Shaken from the daily reality shifting.
Seeing out the window glass,
And seeing confusion deluded with selfish
prideful desires from greedy people.
Mind wired to be the rider of justice.
Finding justice isn't justices anymore, only a
fairytale of who has the biggest payout bills.
I climb some of life's biggest hills, and still am

learning every mountain has many more hills to
it, has many more adventures laying on in me.
Sought out Heavens mountain,
So I know my road of life will never end.
That in the end,
Those once upon time moments are memories
made, that only time can give you.
I space time, seeing any end is only the
beginning to another place in life.
Pacing and placing the moments accordingly,
So each chapter of life can be fulfilled correctly.

[Staged]

The stage is staged.
The battle is won but engaged still.
Wind mill mind running humming.
Twin engines minds tied in line marching.
Launching middle zone targets.
Struggling hustling justifying.
Second guessing wishing nothing.
Wondering if it's doing anything.
Seeking out places,
Sky heavens.
Finding wounded fallen soldiers.
Putting on my armor upping my shoulders and
running in as a warrior standing by Angels.
Undergoing an underdog hero moment.
Finding clarity in the simplest forms.
Slipping in forms of saving grace.
Asking God for more grace.

Walking around with a happy face.
Making life the best I can.
Standing being the man I ran to become.
Looking in a mirror seeing it all clearer.
Seeing life's only getting weirder.
Seeing things even wider.
Wired to connect the puzzle pieces.
Wired the wild child kid genius.
Witness the times fall on beneath us.
Screaming what is this?
How is this?
This isn't what life I signed up for.
Trapped in a time ever faster changing.
Looking over seeing everything all disarranged.
Life's falling apart here and over there.
The poor only getting poorer and rich getting
only richer that it is sicking to witness.
Poor me a drink of tea and sit me back and let
me meditate and think.
Puts me in a deep place.
Seeing through all surfaces and stages.
Up raged on the changing age.
Feel us free falling faster than we know.
Us calling wishing we could go back.
So high up we can't even remember way back.
Came back from seeing the lost fallen future.
All us dead and only a few left standing.
Love dead,
God even deader.
Fade back to see that if God didn't come back.

We wouldn't be alive.
Translating the messages.
Feeling a little restless lately.
Wondering how much more translating got to be
done. Seeing my job isn't ever going to be done
soon. So cuddle in with the new approaching
time and wait.
Hugging my pillow,
Seeing the on coming storm.
Sounding my horns,
And warning all the new borns.
Tossing my hands in the air,
And now whispering,
"Jesus take the wheel.
Let life get real."

[Push On]

Ever have that push?
That motive of motivation of temptation to move
on to that fast line of having it all?
A daily request being tempted.
It's only a devil pray away,
But having to go the other way.
Sized my shoes too big,
Stepped up into those big boy's players game
face shoes too soon it would seem.
Glance over overseeing a demon in the rear
mirror trying to come in.
Wondering who else is near.
Hearing whispers in my ears.

Fearing nothing:
Only of loosing my soul.
After that gold,
After that old told folktales.
Seeing which wishing wheel well has it for me.
Try so hard to keep going forward, But
backwards I seem to go.
Repeating patterns of life keep reappearing in
my driver's rear mirror.
Wondering who else is near.
Steering to the right—
Then to the left—
To the right—
Seeing what else is left?
Trying to shine my hardest launching taking
flight to some unknown place.
Living through the night and day.
Praying everyday for more grace,
Knowing one day it'll all be okay again.
That sin will loose,
And Heaven will win.
For we already know who wins.
Jesus Christ, the Holy Spirit & God.
Seeing the only gold I'm after is in Heaven.
That earthy money and fame is worthless.
Is selfish and only meaningless in the long run.
So praying for forgiveness, hoping the only
riches gained are to support God .
#LoveOn
— Sir Knight Writes—

[Sliding]

Went sliding down a huge hillside.
Gliding over hilly hills—
Snowboarding and flying—
Riding the excitement.
Driving the energy waves,
High-fiving seeing a new tide coming in.
Wondering on about what time?
Seeing times going faster than fast.
Things go in and go out.
Me in, me out.
Finding what life's about.
Seeing it has a lot of repeating factors.
So factoring out that;
Out riding out on a tractor,
With a calculator on a rancher branching out.
Minds spinning thinking how to repent and not
be a sinner, calculating how many sins
committed, seeing too many to even calculate.
The more I dig in inner, the more the sinner
pops out being bigger.
Hand on the trigger of life still trying to battle
out staying alive.
Still high-fiving,
Driving out trying my hardest onto survival.
Understanding there is no surviving here,
Unless love is a part of it.
And God is love.
So reflection period on God must be the solution.

Seeing theres no point in seeing how many sins
have been committed for Jesus forgives me
already. Now I must allow myself to forgive me.

[Dig In]

People look at me:
Ask me this and that.
What did I do?
Create someone who knows everything?
But that isn't possible!
But it is—kind of—
They say something—
I say something—
You saying—
I connect those sayings to understanding—
But wait,
What happens when you don't know?
You look, and search for its answers,
Until it's rugged up, hugged up—
Dug up into placed each-bodies souls
understands clearly.
But what is up—?
When up isn't up no more?
For we no longer no good or evil,
So it would seem—-
Oh you hearing me?
I know you are but aren't you the one looking at
me?
Asking which hand is writing?
And which verse is being said with a clear

understanding of it all?
Do you really know,
Do you,
Do you,
I ask?
Multitasking again—
Here we go again,
Me and You,
Looking loving,
Doing what's up?
What's up—?
Ummm..." I don't know yet,
But we will know soon enough,
So here we wait,
And debate...
"Why wave in this way and that way if the
waving isn't saving?"
Coming running saying words that are so
beautiful lyrically written,
But half spokenly said,
Because it's hard to match its beauty with voice
Wondering if they ever will be said as beautiful
as mentally pictured?
Out ready to figure these things out.
Running out of things to say,
But then suddenly filled with much more to say.
Just sit there and let that mind spin, and it
begins to spin on some more and more.
An engine that soon enough tries to sin again.
What is this friend?

Penning each verb,
Some saying what dude you're some nerd—
Some crazy—
I say,
"Hey—
I'm just trying to be me!
How God made me to be.
Let me be me."
Spinning the mind on to see where it leads.
Praying God directs such spinning for if not, we all know sinning be the ending.
So get it, make God your engine, for we are the wheels spinning.

[Mind]

When the mind wakes:
It makes my mind shake,
Shake, because it's awake.
I wonder if I think more than others, or if it's a soul and spirit differences.
I come close to many a like me but never having the hopeful visions of expanding in finding something better like me.
Never finding a true dreamer;
Only people who think a lot deeper, But their thinking and my thinking are so different that they can never understand what I say fully—
For never in a life time would they have thought what I thought, so it seems.
Leaving me haunting with why me, Why am I so different?

Who's my company?
I know I'm never alone,
Even if alone I feel all the time,
I'm not.
Maybe am I some fallen star follower hollering
after the devil.
For more evil dwells in my life than God some
days it would seem.
I seek God and speak of God,
But do I have Him as my company?
How could I be such a player on both sides and
love both so much?
How's that possible?
Is it I still fight with Good & Evil,
Within my very soul?
I know who to hate,
For I know what fate will be to all who betake of
the forbidden fruit.
Which is surely death.
So God please save me from me.
For I choose You, saying, evil flee for you are no
longer welcome by me, for I am protected by the
Almighty.
Amen.
— Sir Knight Writes—

[Low Days]

When those down low depressed moments hit—
Best take a double take of it all.
Once hitting that wall,
You best start calling out to all and any.

Some days I feel like I'm some mini dude chilling
fading away.
Wondering which gateway is me?
Wondering why life has to be the way it is?
Play it good—
Do it good—
Seeing nothing—
So back to that back scatter life I run.
Running as a runner never getting any dumber
only smarter.
Calling out Father—
Why can't you come and make all this pain fade
away from me?
I live that righteous life and find I have no true
lasting long friends.
Back down trapped into a whole other type of
den. Seeing me this way feeling at least
something—But the pain that comes in,
It hurts—!
Wondering who's watching listening to this
verse. Already knowing many are,
But why aren't you?
When I needed you then,
Where were yeah?
Me off limits,
I know—
It'll always be this way.
Only me and you,
And you will get it!
Everyone else never will,

Not completely.
Because they can't!
If they did,
They would be freaking out of the true reality
they live in.
In prison here,
Feeling like nothing I do is ever right.
See the creeping night getting extra something.
Full moons bigger than ever,
Now smaller than ever,
Yet it's something normal.
For science says it's so.
Leaving us still sponging off anything—
Me asking:
What do you feel within your very soul?
Are things right?
Do what I say spark light within you?

[Alive Soul]

The soul alive:
The mind aligned:
The heart bottomed lined.
The soul's song survives on;
The minds spinning on to the beat of the hearts
pitter patting patterns.
Each flowing on blood gauge determining
another emotional level.
Raising up the soul to the heavenly clouds.
Fly up mind to align.
Heart pitter pat just that much harder.

The souls alive living:
The mind spinning,
Again and again—
All awhile the heart bottomed lined in aligning
to it all.
But how?

[Greatest Battle]

You have those moments;
You want to toss yourself back onto that pulpit.
Saying man, I'm tired of this and want to quit it.
So sit back down I do;
I do what I do because I'm glued to you.
I was taught in this life way view to be this way.
What do you mean boo?
I'm saying I'm no zombie freak out about me to
speak about you.
Sober I do and stay so candy fresh containing a
steady brain.
Somedays feeling like I'm insane.
Kingdoms sway instilling in the steel feel.
Playing picky boo—
Little boo you I still missing you.
Me almost tearing up wondering if I still feeling
blue?
Showering in fresh robes.
Taking the hate ropes and tossing away them at
the cross of Jesus—
At Jesus's feet next to the thief.
Feeling a major sense of grief.

Deep underneath death rolling up next to me
trying to pull me back betting with me about my
beliefs.
Seeking out up high to the sky to the heavens—
Asking the universe questions about my
testimonial versus wondering if I'm truly am
cursed or blessed?
Letting emotions of negativity come in
overpowering the positivity causing a mess.
Me hearing voices saying you're a survival of
reality gist.
You can beat your rivals holding on to the Holy
Bibles gravity lists.
Gravel traveling swiftly.
As in being grounded in sound judgment,
stumbling on everything in between in life so it's
close to me so I understand.
The man I used to be was six feet under beneath
head deep in the sand.
Now I dig out—
Ring out with myself freely out holding my
hands out to all trying to help.
Telling everyone what I'm about.
Trying to drop the pride and ride in on love.
Taking the Oceans and sea tides seeing new
horizons.
Starting to see the new light to all things.
Finding purpose and meaning to everything
with real reasons.
Heart out hopping on living loving off positivity

bringing in new beautiful views.
Sky blue skies fall upon my eyes.
Any lies I see—
Now I know how to dodge.
Anytime in arguments now I know how to
pause.
Know when and how to applause.
So dodge ball I play.
Sailing away in life feeling alive.
Feeling the battle firing bullets right at me.
Live Free or Die Hard Trying Giving Peace to All
whispers on among the bullets.
You have those moments;
You want to toss yourself back onto that pulpit.
Saying man, I'm tired of this and want to quit it.
Wondering always when your messages will be
done and over with, For you try drawing the fine
line to this life and find what's divine.
But your mind never stops recording them
messages for the present times.
Each step you take you're being tested.
Feeling like you're in a wrestling match.
A fire match ready to be lit on fire.
Finding each hardship that comes your way as a
new way for new inspiration.
Viewing life in all aspects.
Injected to be some Sir,
Sir Protector.
Some Sir Knight.
Projected as some Sir Protector Knight on a big

screen universal projector.
Rejected by most predictors.
Shaving using a razor to have an appearance
that's seen as ready for a performance.
Gifted with having a beloved charm.
To be armed and alarmed to any coming harm.
Farmer boy raised but ready in arms carved.
The guy with the right words at the right time
curved.
A smiling picture holding card living motto.
Pronto on time with delivering what needs to be
served.
A deep down at heart nerd.
Trying to be pure with God with my right-hand
actions.
Putting passion and compassion behind every
motion before each given action.
Examining each and every question and
suggestion imaginable.
Wondering if I'm still capable of holding out onto
the Golden Rules faithfully.
Stable condition giving me new situation of
rationality capturing its chaos mixed with
beauty that's beautiful.
Why you say that blissfully?
Because each time I'm thrown down and try to
be brought to have a frown—
I'm given a bigger golden crown.
Father of Earth lies' calling me down,
Down,

Down,
To download a new mission but Private Eye Sir
comes in asking praying who's prey you trying
to haunt?
Me, haha me?
No—
God protects me
Projects and directs me.
No never you again—
We can play picky boo all day long and still see
at the end of the day which song is sung.
Which bell is rung?
Until I'm done we are fighting all the time
having a timeline prime time fun machine gun
battle.
It may get outta control—
But in control I can be with my emotions better
than most.
For training has been committed.
Demons fighting with a human,
A soon to be an angelic prince—
And because of this you are hating me satan.
Trying your hardest to make me fall my hardest
and longest.
But forgetting I find it all to be the loveliest.
You're helping me to become my strongest.
Roger roger Sir Knight ringing over.
Angels saying dodge,
Dodge,
Now charge!

My Mirrors Reflection

Charge, charge full force ahead!
Sometimes my connection to heaven getting
interrupted by my own corruption and I head
down my own direction.
God coming calling in saying get back on course
Here's the correctional reasons to why your way
wasn't so fashionable, But emotionally rash.
Now go fast correcting yourself back into the
right direction for there is only one direction
and pathway for eternity life.
So life sits,
And you think in,
And on,
Wondering on which song is being rung?
You look at me,
And say,
Boy,
You say this,
Say that,
But are you truly that,
And that!?
Me stepping in,
Saying I set standards and goals, Trying to
reach them.
So reach them I do,
I try,
I keep motivated on going after that passion.
Anyone laughing,
You asleep sleeping,
When I been thinking to vision,

Mentioning some life here in these pages.
You have those moments you wan to fall back;
But within those moments, actions happen,
Battling trying to better keeps on talking.
So walking on having those moments.
Praying to God to lead all the way in this life of:
Live Free or Die Hard Trying Giving Peace to
All.
God fearing—
Asking for forgiveness—
But sometimes loose site into this world's
concept of living—
Shying off from the Holy Bibles words.
Finding then bitterly,
How sour this world truly is.
So falling back on track—
Steady head raised high looking forward to my
Master.
Bowing my head,
Worshiping my King.
Forever & ever.
Knowing I'm only the messenger.
#LoveOn
— Sir Knight Writes—

[Coming Days]

Days of crazy are coming,
Are you ready?
Mayday of devils preying,
Gods angels delaying,

Praying.
Days of crazy are coming,
Are you ready?
Decreasing mindsets on human mankind
towards sickness that brings in wickedness
playing its games,
Displaying its decay.
Days of crazy are coming,
Are you sure you're ready?
Bible in hand knees down praying.
Last days sounding it sounds,
Last days sounding it sounds.
Round one, two, three, four.
Four winds blowing,
All four traveling around everyone's soul.
Seeking the seekers,
Requesting more time,
Just please a little bit more.
More souls at stake,
Wait wait wait! —
Days of crazy are coming,
Are you sure you're ready?
For it's those days.
Those days' people have been waiting for
centuries.
Last days,
End of times days.
What do you say?
Do you see the signs?
— **Sir Knight Writes**—

[Gray Days]

We all go through those bad days,
Those gray ones.
We feel like life is sucking us downward.
Feeling gloominess with sadness when
emotionally depressed levels hit.
Gray sky days with rain making it feel even
worst at times, to sometimes being peaceful.
Wondering if the next verse will elevate or
devastate?
So double take of the data you do.
We all go through those bad days,
Meaning you're not alone.
We feel like life is sucking us downward meaning
life is expanding our tolerance level.
Feeling gloominess with sadness when
emotionally depressed levels hit—
Meaning you need to look to more of the
positivity in life,
And those feelings will go away.
Wondering if the next verse will elevate or
devastate,
Meaning you choose what will happen—!
Choose who you wanna be,
And become it!
You wear what you sow.
As in—
Your actions and choices ultimately tell it all.

[Crystal Blue]

Crystal blue clear blue skies resting upon my
eyes.
Clouds sliding by,
Saying,
"Hello, how do you do?"
Crystal blue clear blue skies resting upon my
eyes.
Surprised by each sparkling sun ray,
By each passing on day.
Crystal clear visions.
Seeing each one as something special.
Over beyond-yonder under a tree on a sunny
day,
Day dreaming of crystal blue clear blue skies,
While I simply just rest my eyes.
Wishing I had God eyes.
To fully see even more beauty that lays beyond
those crystal clear blue skies heavens.

[Light]

Even in those moments of darkness—
Something always stays on lighting your
pathway keeping you shining on.
Once focus and determination to push on goes
on through your mind;
It makes you stand up,
Head out of the sand—
Demanding justification and actions to past
down done lowering on pitter patter bad plans

you had —
That battered you—
Splattered you down to rock bottom realities—
You now spinning upward with God as your rock
Making new visions towards your reality—
That's gladder, you now wiser from such
foolishness back in those 'down done lowering
on pitter patter pattern bad days'.
Happier now —
Being some Sir Gladiator Alligator Protector for
justest—
Now we pray dear God,
Please add me onto some latter rain,
So we can be some spokesperson to help out
those who can't!
Even in those dark moments,
There is light.
So fight the night,
And fight any darkness with the light of
righteousness.

[Miles Walked]

I walk miles a day these days.
Never getting a chance to think
Though,
Only pacing on,
And on.
Walking those long halls,
Reaching up those tall walls shelves searching
finding someone's goodies.

Getting a second to plunder on why someone
would be buying this and that—
Then looking at a scanner seeing a banner
saying,
"Hey boy,
Move on to the next bin.
Deep within pushing on,
To mile seven,
Not thinking a bit.
Getting sick how screwed up the world gotta be
That someone could go spend 10 hours without
a bit of a time to sit really,
Just so you can have something sooner than
later.
After work,
My elevator of thoughts rushes in.
Wishing that the time spent was more
productive towards actual life,
Thinking to the positive;
Knowing you just knocked out many miles
easily, smiling always feeling cheesy,
Seeing just how greedy and self-needy people
have become.
Seeing deeper within sin city reality floating on.
Wondering on—
Why doesn't something happen by now.
It's been beyond time, right?
I see within in,
Future—
Seeing the time as precious,

But wonder why doesn't it hit me harder with
truly how precious it is?
Questioning life mattering matters.
Going on in those life long trails,
Walking those miles still thinking on about life.
For life is that important.
That the many miles we walk regular less,
They all add up to one finally decisioning point,
Which is choosing which gates we will walk into,
Deaths or Eternal Life's?

[Door Open]

When that door opens,
You take it.
You pray dear Lord,
Retake, relook and then book.
Maybe you will feel that hesitation on in going
on moving forward.
But once that footstep goes on,
Moves on,
Keeps on heading for that goal,
That mission, etc. forward—
You see progress,
See visions coming into reality,
See growth,
New realities,
And see life is what you make it.
Understanding this is only a nutshell,
So best sure make it the best you can,
Keeping God close—

Keeping life moving on smoothly.
Knowing risky it may be at times,
But soul in line,
Mind on some goals,
New ideas, friends, relations, making life as
awesome as it gets—
Never forgetting how blessed I am,
How much bloodshed was lead for such—
Never getting enough of its blessings,
Always thanking America and God for another
day of blessings of living freely.
Never seeing less in anything but as much as
possible in everything as I can.
Taking heavenly given wisdom and God given
wisdom and sharing it with my peers.
Trying to give us all some cheers,
Making life an example of positivity.
Wanting to change the world,
But feel I must change me first,
So my next verse,
Next example,
Can be that channel for someone to want to
change to be someone more loving.
Disarranged at times—
Trying not to change with the new times.
Feel demons present with Angels nearby
battling out our personal fights,
Making each day and night intensify.
Testifying my demons are real,
Feel them nearby at times,

But God even nearer.
Seeing Heaven now clearer.
So when that door opens,
You take it after praying first,
But after thinking of actual life.
What shall your next verse say?
Mine will say,
"Forever Love On"
"Living Free or Dying Hard Trying,
Giving Peace to All."
#LoveOnForever

[Thanksgiving]

I open my eyes thankful for another day,
Surprised I was given another day of living to
rise and see nature still breathing on.
Today is Thanksgiving,
But everyday should be a day of thanks of
giving to God for what He has done for us.
Some wonder how they can be so thankful:
I am broke,
I am sick,
I am at my darkest place imaginable,
Full of disappointments,
Struggling along here to the next day.
Blinding themselves from the seen blessings
that where given to them that very day.
You were given another day to choose to make a
difference.
A day of given sunshine,

Fresh air,
Beautiful sky miles,
People smiling their smiles,
Mile long pathways that lead to places for you to
experience new wonders and sights.
A known fact of salvation at your finger tip
footsteps if you choose God to lead you on.
You can step your steps into that doorstep—
Into that doorway of heavenly blessings—
To a known way of true ever lasting happiness.
Having visions of pure positive attitudes forever
Having attentive attention towards heavens air.
Leaving each day a living day of love to tell all.
An everyday of giving of Thanksgiving to life.
A day to spend with family and those you love,
To make it our duty to be happy no matter what
For God, Jesus, and the Holy Spirit truly are
alive at work to take our hell given realities
away, and place in there still blessings of
awesomeness! Refilling us everyday;
Leaving everyday an awesome day of praying to
God repeating over and over
Happy Thanksgiving!
#LoveOn.
— Sir Knight Writes—

[You're A Love Song]

Loves like a game.
You have to jump up and play it.
Say to it, "Baby, love,
Love me;

Me love me for me.
I gotta play lucky picky boo,
I'm superglued to me."
See me in the morning,
In the mirror it's Jesus and me,
It's clear I must love me.
For Jesus does.
Take what I am,
And either fix it—
Change or accept and grow and become
someone home grown deep down in your DNA—
Sworn to make yourself the best you can.
Stand up, holding your hands up praying,
Demanding for love from above to come into
you, to say hey maybe I can love me—
Yeah me—!
See me, In the mirror,
It's simply Jesus and me.
It's clear,
I must love me.
So see,
Love, love,
So you can be set free from your prison den
within—
Somedays you may wake up,
And say,
"Man.....I hate today!"
Look at me!
Yes, stupid me look!
Why did you just do that!

My Mirrors Reflection

Take that bat and hit that smack whack crack
head up,
Because life's pissing me off!
Yeah, I'm going off into the third person,
Committing treason upon myself!
I look and see my hair,
And ask how it fair?
I see super models and see their hair so pretty!
Forgetting it takes them 4 hours to get that
tower of some hair firepower to be ready!
Open the door and bam, wam,
It's like I get hit by everything,
Stub my toe,
and almost want to let go,
and say no more, no more,
But maybe there is more?
I'm not that torn;
Maybe I can redo my day.
And say hey,
Today will be my hero super day!
Her-Ray,
Yay! —
I see light rays of sunshine,
Yes, that's me shining,
Coming smiling,
Saying today will be something better!
I may look like crap,
My hair is a wreck,
But screw it! —
My inside air is on going to the positivity,

Taking that to make my reality not hate,
But oh howdy mate,
Let me ring off my outgoing side of cheerfulness
Dodging those haters—
Those being fakes and snakes—
I'm retaking remaking myself organized—
An original and some superhero—
Some superman—!
So listen!
God is love,
So I am loved,
period.
(Hook)
Fly, fly, fly, fly away to a new day.
Love, love, love becoming my new way.
Fly, fly, fly, fly away to a new day.
Love, love, love, for there's no other way.
Fly, fly, fly, fly to love, for it's the only way.
Love, love onwards her-ray-ya-yay!
Here goes another day,
Down low,
Day seems to be so slow!
Almost feel like letting it go!
Talking taking that bottle and making it
disappear, because it's the way I feel!
Feel like I been in a mill grinding almost dying!
But why,
Oh yes why!?
Why would I feel like dying!
Get ready to listen!

My Mirrors Reflection

Come into my life!
Down so low,
I can't even hold myself to control from not
letting it go!
I poor those tears,
Making my own swimming pool,
Any who think it's cool to pick on me,
Screw you,
You devil used tool!
I gotta try on a daily to keep my cool!
Open up that Holy Book and try to get any
translations to its Revelations pages—
But all I seem to get is more rages,
From not understand these pages!
Why,
Why must I still cry!
Why oh why can't I open my eyes and fly to
those skies!
Dropping these lies about myself,
Because I'm important,
I'm beautiful,
I'm loved,
I can love me,
Because look at me,
Once this gloom moves,
I see rivers of passion for doing actions of love.
So don't you dare get in my run, runway!
Because I'm ready,
Ready to, what what—!
(Hook)

Fly, fly, fly, fly away to a new day.
Love, love, love becoming my new way.
Fly, fly, fly, fly away to a new day.
Love, love, love, for there's no other way.
Fly, fly, fly, fly to love, for it's the only way.
Love, love onwards her-ray-ya-yay!

[Wake Up]

You wake up feeling free.
Wake up wanting to believe all is alright.
You look and double look to the right and then
to the left to make sure it's clear before pulling
out your driveway.
Diving in on traffic, praying to God that nothing
tragic happens.
The devil comes in trying to play some magic.
Tapping trying to do a mind kidnapping.
You snapping battling hard to break that habit.
And snapping back at it; demanding no more
mild middle ground fiddling.
It's about time; to take that stand on the Holy
Grounds across all boards of our life's.
Most of us wake up thinking what's next?
At the fence leaning while trying to do a
cleaning of life up.
Trying to come up with a new pathway to say
hey man this way is what's up.
By the time the engine mind is warmed up,
We end up doing nothing but foolish thinking.
By midday,

The thought re-enters but we pretend it didn't.
It's stressing testing making our best engines
tick tock on the clock almost mocking.
Our minds end up rewinding back in time,
Forward,
Annoyed-words to the awkward moments
winning mad awards to the prison doors trying
to do a locking.
Wondering what made things so crazy?
Driving you nuts,
But you saying there are no buts to this mess
up. By 4 o'clock it hits,
Yeah,
Wondering why it took yah so long,
Feeling like you went somewhere wrong all day,
And sung the wrong song so the ding dong door
bell rings.
Mind alerts pop in saying man, dude—
What you thinking your mind engine going to do
when you forget about putting God into your
planes first?
Now let's start over with a new verse.
God first, putting yourself way fist away.

[Sit & Listen]

While I sit and try to listen in hard to hear
anything back.
I try to ask for permission to understand
heaven a little bit more asking God to give me a
little slack.
God comes back giving me a pat on the back

saying relax son I am always here.
If I can make an ax float back to the surface isn't
that showing you a little of Heaven?
If I can come and take a sinner and turn them
into a heavenly winner,
Isn't that Me working in your life on the inner?
Sometimes it hard to see how God works in our
lives, but He is always working.
Always coming in and adding something to our
life to help us understand Him a little better—
To even understand ourselves better.
Making us have a daily homework to reflect on
each morning.
To see back onto yesterday and see all the
blessings He gave us.
Sometimes we let the past rush in and push in
onto our rusty negativity—
Pulling us down into a reality that isn't true.
What is true is God always loves us,
Always turns our blues into rainbow colors of
light to shine onto others—
To help others turn away from such a downer
tone into a happier one.
It's everything we been through in life that
makes us who we are and who we will become.
Some of us have been down into low pits and
others haven't been down as low,
But within each journey,
We go down,
God is always there trying to guide us back

home up home to Heaven.
Even if we choose to go down a pathway that
isn't so great,
God is still always there waiting to help you but
also then to turn those bad moments into
blessings for others to become truly great.
Some question and ask God if they truly have
any meaning into His larger picture of helping of
saving souls?
The answer is simple:
We all are as precious as gems and gold,
But even more so—
Our words can't even express how precious we
truly are to God.
If we live and ask God to unfold His love onto us,
into us, we can shine Gods love onto others.
Within doing that,
That in itself is what can make the difference to
someone.
By showing a smile,
By doing a kind gesture,
It's helping to paint a picture of Gods love onto
others.
The highest calling we all can take hold of is
living a God fearing life—
Forgiving forever, loving also forever—
Reflecting His reflection of Jesus Christ
character.
It's our actions that make us stand out.
It's our everyday living that shows to others

who we are as a person.
The question that we all must ask on a daily is:
Will we invite God into our life's today,
So we can display Gods love onto others,
So they too can see a little heaven within us,
And be so encouraged and curious that they ask
us what makes us so different?
That we can't help but smile,
And say it's because God dwells within our very
soul that we smile and are the way we are—
For I know that I am loved and cared for to the
upmost because Jesus died to save me,
And you, that I can't help but shine off His love;
His blessings He has given to me.
At the end of the day we can't loose hope of
heaven, but gain more hope of heaven by having
heaven begin to start growing in our hearts
today.

[Life Passes]

Life grabs one and tosses.
I'm like oh,
Okay,
Dodge, dodge—
Dodge ball I play,
Oh hey, oh okay,
This road seems okay.
Float down the road playing,
Cruising, amusing, snoozing,
Then reintroducing.

Stop signs ringing in trying to say son stop your
playing, but the emotions keep saying on your
playing, so waving in saying okay,
Okay, I'll do some playing;
Comes in swaying.
Motives of influence pop in proving a black
hidden ridden paving.
Within signs still appearing,
Mirroring side affects paging in bloody paying.
But overriding happens,
A mind kidnapping of reason comes in; —
Saying reject side effects.
At intersections intercepting interpretations,
Looking to see which next be the direction to
take.
Life grabs one and tosses,
And I fiddle to figure it out,
And once I do,
I keep moving forward.
Loving,
Sharing kindness.
Looking up,
Hoping Gods backing the whole way.
For I no longer see any other way.

[Broken Connection Reconnected]

I feel bad;
No I feel sad.
I can't say I know anyone of you anymore.

Can't say that you know me either.
There's many of us.
Meaning we should be many strong,
Having our own song,
But's what wrong?
We never made that song,
We somehow missed out on family-hood,
friendship-hood and became our own self's,
Independent individuals.
Which I respect fully,
Don't get me wrong.
But it's sad we never tried to get together and be
together and make some promises to help make
us our strongest.
Yes,
We love each other so we are supposed to,
But the question is why?
Have we forgotten what love is?
Oh, we are family, we are friends—
But what does that even mean?
I see families all the time,
I see inner connected friendships—
And then look back at mine and see us all as
strangers,
But why I ask?
I dig deep.
Perhaps it all was just me pushing away,
But that was only after I gave up on everyone,
Now regathering the puzzle pieces seeing what
went wrong.

See us back as kids,
Playing,
Trying to build damns,
Shooting the bow, throwing the ball, racing
down the road—
Chancing after butterflies and lighten bugs.
And it bugs me,
As the years past on....
We began to push for our own self's meaning and
purpose, in doing so fading away from one
another slowly and slowly till we are strangers.
Remembering back to when we would go into
the woods to try and see which trail should be
next made for the go-carts, which fort to build,
which next game should be played—
Most of us did,
Yet many of us already too busy to even think
about such.
Having our axes and knives thinking we were so
cool, being little old us.
While others at work, working away.
Actually having actual conversations of
expressing what we thought of in a deeper way.
Seeing already how I was being pushed away
because I always tried to be just like everyone
else, but started to keep expressing myself more
and more — getting deeper and deeper, so being
seen more and more as 'different'
Now I would never want to be in any since of the
word as the 'same', 'normal', 'regular' —what

does that even mean anyways, robotically
acceptable by society?
Because it made me fall so many times that it
makes it easy to not want that.
To even say this.
I come back,
Crying saying I did all I could in trying to be a
part of what everyone else was doing—
I just adding my touch of me to it all, but didn't
you too?
Voices whispering in,
Saying don't listen to them,
You can shine alone,
But me coming in saying alone I don't wanna be,
But maybe you're right.
Back now inside with my brothers inside our
room playing cars.
Me always trying to one up what their
imaginations had coming,
But still being pushed,
Me so young always wondering why I couldn't
be a part of what they were doing.
Heart-sickening to even think about,
But head high strong thinking to solve.
Wondering what could I have done to be more
likable by everyone?
Even tried not being myself to be accepted as
'acceptable,' but the deeper me kept pushing out
My one brother always trying to be in charge
and I could tell that,

So I saw him as my biggest competitor,
Another being so chilled never saying much but
always agreeing to the point he could say
something and nobody would question him.
So respect we all had to give him.
Me personally,
Never understood a single thing about the oldest
beside he liked fishing,
Snakes and reptiles and cars and landscaping.
That's all I could file him as.
Making me ask myself do I even know him?
Leaving the biggest question, he never cared to
know about me, actions shown that over and
over, leaving mixed feelings to develop.
Should I even try to remember him in a file?
Drink some more I think I should do, as of now,
Why because for me it's a dark place I have to go
to even say anything of this.
Which is messed up,
It should be a happy place,
But no, it's painful, drinking doesn't help, I
know, but hey i'm still on my demon stretch of
recovery, knowing drinking only invites them in
more, probably why it messes with me so much,
for many times again it has ruined me, made me
want to hate, but God getting me wiser.
Making me ask even more to why things had to
be the way they were?
Now we are in a new place.
A place where we all are only growing more

apart, actions show that over and over.
Me at heart having to start slowly falling in love
with purely only myself.
Why because I was so pushed away by you all
that it's discussing to dwell on.
Me pushing for years to be just like you,
But now me finally being able to break off onto
myself and not even feel bad about it.
Becoming a person that has so many shadows
that it's hard to even express.
A man that has so many sides that I can't even
hide—so saddling them all together, combining
transforming powers from God, putting myself
together slowly, knowing the day I'm brave
enough to show myself, many will never know
what's coming, for I had to hide that much of
me. Years later,
Someone telling me hey,
You will be fine,
Because you are a loner.
Me remembering that daily,
Faithfully saying they are right.
Now hating myself for believing such lies,
Falling back upon nothing but the Bible now.
Saying God loves us all—
But me asking what does that even mean?
Yes, I know,
I truly do,
But why can't I relate,
Why can't I understand love?

Is it I been so damaged and pushed that love
isn't even real to me?
So satan's lies come in being real?
Me finally at the point of hiding everything—
To the point I am talking to death.
By the time you know it's been years,
Why because I never had a genuine relationship
with anyone, only myself, for only I could deal
with me, everyone shown over and over they
never could handle me,
It's that simple.
Until this day many of us still don't have a
genuine relationship with anyone, why?
How do you know how I feel even now?
It's simple,
You don't because you never cared to.
Which makes me want to cry because
I am fault to the utmost.
It's why I spill all my heart out now because I
think if I die, or fall,
At least someone should understand my pain,
My view,
And know I truly tried in all ways to reach out.
Now the question is,
Will you be silence and say something simple,
Or reach out into your own hearts and say
something from the heart.
To make me understand your life and your love.
Because I love you all,
But it's hard for me to even say why.

Because it's hard to know why which is sad.
But somehow I do,
And I am only being honest.
I have only told my mom I loved her when I was
drunk, why,
Because I was afraid,
But moreover,
I only half know what that means.
Meaning, I love you,
But I can't say I even fully know what that
means besides expecting and accepting
everything with love,
But I never told my dad I loved him because I
honestly don't even know if I could.
Like I love dad,
But understand him and me have been to some
dark places:
Leaving new growth to develop and take place
in us all.
So all of this can change,
Transforming into everlasting love.
Only if we seek it.
Cherish it.
Own it and live it!
We can become it!
Unfolding the past for what it was,
Knowing now after reviewing these past
moments years later to more present days,
God has stepped in, syncing relations, sobering
me up, revealing more each day what love truly

means. Leaving me each time now when I say I love you all, the understanding goes deep, leaving these words aren't ever said lightly, but with years of struggling moments to understand it all was needed so I could express what love truly even means. — #LoveOn

[Off Rhyme]

Ever have those times when your mind doesn't rhyme right or chime what you think it should?
You look at the time and see it ticking and within that you wish you would feel something good within besides nothingness.
Asking yourself why are you feeling so lonely?
Homie self-stepping in asking why you feeling so phony?
Each morning waking up,
Saying you are not going to town today,
But own and join in on something funny.
So out on trying to do something lovely
You doing it swiftly.
Writing historical notes down in these pages.
Some may and try and call me crazy,
But I'm just expressing how life has affected me,
How it affects us all.
Saying really,
Each day we choose to do what we do.
We can do more,
Or do the same.
We choose.
Each day is a new day.

Each day something new can happen.
You can learn,
Reach out and test it then—
I'm always studying more,
So I can tell everyone more.
How about you?
You off rhyme or on rhyme?

[Something in the Air]

Why do I feel better after hearing something
crazy?
It's like I feel the energy within the crazy.
It's wild;
I'm a wild kid,
But look in the mirror now and can't see that
person anymore clearly.
Deep down knows he's still there,
That this serious boy can't be fully here yet.
Double check and wonder why my emotions are
rock solid and wonder why it takes a rocket for
them to come to life?

Devil
Shot shot creeps in my mind somedays,
Saying, "Hey boy a shot will fix this rough edge
seriousness."

Recovery self
Perhaps; but we know what happens once I take
a shot,
It's like shot shot shot shot shot POP it's 9
o'clock.
Locked out in space pacing and wondering what

I did.
At first,
I felt better,
Felt the stress lift,
Felt the crazy-ness come.
At first a good crazy,
I'm talking a crazy where you feeling daisies
and smiley faces.
It's like a fake amazing grace.
You end up wishing you now baked up high;
I'm looking down on the sky night past days.
Remember them clearly,
Feel them nearly.
Know I got away from the devil,
But dove into a gas chamber where it's just me
still as lonely as I once was so it feels.
Why that gotta be?
Knowing it's because I still focus on the past,
seeing I need to stop.

Devil

"Homie, yes yes you you homie.
Do you leave me?
Or do you believe me?"

Faded self:

I see happy trees.
Feeling happiness wearing a halo saying hello
homie.
I'm not a zombie;
I'm an underdog nicer on boxer.
A look at me lion fox—.

Na I'm not bossy,
I'm just coasting on becoming lostly, lusty.
Angel
Costly said words pop in my head.
God:
Why you becoming brain dead insane— with
dumber on changing on things?
You wish you could feel crazy,
But why?
Clarity's better.
Sweet said things of wisdom is like honey.
Devil
That's funny!
That's something only a dummy would say.
Angel
But no no it's not!
God
It's like a hot box of chocolates melting when
you are saying you want some crazy.
It's like a warm bed of lovely when you say hello
wisdom.
You say you in a prison?
A prison of what?
A drink of poison is a prison not mentioning a
sin, so think again my friend on who be winning
when you thinking friend is your evil twin.
Past Lost Self: devil accompanied
Smile,
Yes, yes it's me back.
It's whack,
But just think about it,

You did what today?
Think about me all day, almost.
A ghost came back from the past to say what
cost does it cost for a lost son to come back?
We toss anything imaginable your way.
Anything pleasurable and haunting.
Don't matter where you go we go to.
Think about it,
The other day I know you felt me.
The dogs would be barking,
But when I came,
They stopped.
Why you thinking about at night,
You can't sleep?
Why do you think Christian anything is driving
you nuts?

God

Look look, times running out;
You can't be going this way and that way.

Confused Self

You know what!
I'll go one way and in my own way of
going—
Then you all coming talking to me,
you come haunting and barking back at me like
that.
Look at me when I am talking!
I go after God and feel this moment of
something.
Maybe I'm not trying hard enough; I'm talking I

am out looking thinking about God,
Then this idea of me being God still steps in my
mind! But why all these negative self related
thoughts?

Angel

Probably another demon whispering. Pray to
God, begone all demons, God will answer.

Recovery self

I look at things and feel something, but why?
I feel evil surrounds me more than heavenly
things.
I'm addicted to music, but the music I think is
suitable is depressing.
Pressing on down till done gone.
Wait stop;
I listen to good magic,
Wait I mean music,
But it's magic.
Black magic it's tragic you light a match and
watch it burn.
Leaving time to do the unthinkable.
As in the magic is the suggestions;
Such power of over powering suggestions that
they come into reality as time passes.
In the sense, the suggestions help you see life's
realities, thus in a lot of aspects can interfere
with your decision making, this applies to all
media. See there is good music,
Then there is bad music.
Most music today isn't acceptable in my eyes,
For most is foolish, sexual, self empowering, and

meaningless.

So be wise with what you choose to listen to,
what you watch, so much more could be said,
but try to listen to music that empowers your
soul, is uplifting towards the positive, that talks
about God, that doesn't make you angry, etc.

Music is very powerful, very very so.

God

For I know the time we live in.

The confusion,

And mixed ideas and delusions—

Open My Word.

Read My Words—

The Bible enlightens you better than any book
imaginable.

For the lessons and words still speak for today.

I am coming very soon.

Why not love Me?

When all I have done for you is love you as you,

No matter where you have been.

I love you,

And will forever love you.

But I can only let the justice enter into My
gates.

For no hate, crime, pride, or fallen thing can
ever be entered in.

The Grace I have is much.

All I seek is your heart.

Do you accept Jesus, accept Me?

Try Me,

I Am Love.
Understanding all.
Seek wisdom and I shall give you it.
Seek love, and love shall be yours.
— God

[Confusion]

Sometimes we struggle on in life.
Forgetting painful memories,
But faced with new problems, knife at the neck.
Upset over things,
Questioning which message was supposed to be
said; In check.
Wishing that wasn't said that you weren't so
stupid in the head way back.
Feeling a heavy drink some days would do the
trick. But see it as a dark trick,
A sticker bush thorn.
A Devils push me on to destruction song horn.
Feel my wrongs come in creeping.
Know I'm free—
But still seeing evils face in the mirror peeking.
Steering the other way speaking, dear God.
Looking up to heaven and asking why am I lost
here alone in zone by monsters?
Dumpster mind spinning sin coming in penning.
Demons hiding and appearing drilling.
Angels above hovering covering my insanity.
Reality creeping in,
Sleeping with Gods hedge of protection knowing

soon pledges of destruction will happen.
Tapping my toes and smelling with my noise
good mixed in with bad.
Seeing a lad hungry and feel sad.
Trying to help a tad and feel glad.
Gladiator Sir Protector Witnesser of black
abysses so dark that it spark sadness and pain
into heartbrokenness—
Falling back towards the Holy Spirits Ark of
Righteousness that it's Christ-like in human
form.
What do you mean before a storms formed?
Came back from the darkest places imaginable
now try shining off Christ character—
Finding the true meaning to how our Creator is
our forever Savior Number One Team Supporter
Our only way towards salvations dream—
The A-Z Air Plane Plan that can take my
insanity pain away and turn that into
something useful;
So it wasn't vain.
Brain feelin' like it's dripping blood type of pain.
Flooded with ideas and knowledge of love mixed
in with sipping of black wine sin shame.
But to truly understand loves hand you first got
to respect it.
To fully understand evils game, you have to just
open your eyes and look at society.
But to respect it you have to go through all
aspects of loves hand to see it's importance to

protect it.
To understand evils game, we have to travel
back in time and see evils faces throughout it all
to learn or live in it for its wild rides with
bloodshot red-eyes.
To see its true lying eyes once God opens our
eyes, so open your eyes to Heaven.
If you been through both,
You can reflect it out and know how to reach
anyone for you have felt sins all;
Its fallen fall—
You can now seek all who have fallen before it's
too late to take Gods calling.
Gods knocking saying stop your mocking.
Devils coming in trying to do a hate heart lock
locking.
People flocking docking into hells doorways.
Me seeing people wishing they could flee,
Yelling: "Look at me—
Why didn't you help me?
Tell me about its realities?"
I head down saying,
"But I did,
I tried but had to leave head down crying
because you didn't care to listen.
Didn't give me permission to do a quick kiss
fixing.
Me wishing something could happen to fix its
sickness.
Praying to God asking for more power to do a

miracle to rewind time to try harder.
Say, fathers, mothers, why didn't we all try
harder?"
Waking up sweating realizing it was a dream
used as a wake-up weapon.
Taking a shower washing off its message.
Hoping its seeds fall correctly,
So listen to reason.
Before committing treason.
For we must have a real reason to live on going
forward, and that reason is God, is love, not
things of this world, it never has been.
Heaven has riches, has peace, and forever
loving gestures, with green pastures, lushes
rivers, waterfalls, mountain views, plus so much
more that words can't even describe its beauty.
Heaven having forever ending places of
unknown unimaginable things,
Only thing we need to know is that Heaven will
be perfect, beyond our understanding perfect.
That you won't even be able to breathe once you
see its realness in person.
That this confusion we live in now is only
temporary.
Look to Heaven, not to this fallen world.
#LoveOn

[Isaiah 2]

Is all about God calling upon us to live loyal to
Him. To not put our trust in men but in Him. It's
more talking about how Israel was told in

advance what they were supposed to do, which was to build a temple, the temple of Jerusalem, which in return God would bless them. All nations would come to them, but they failed and instead fell into sin, and into the things of the world. Slowly they started to worship idols and began to do witchcraft.

Have we ourselves done this in our generation? Have we failed God and done what the past has done and created our own idea and form of God? Have we become a part of satan's work to destroy all of mankind without realizing it? You see the book of Isaiah almost being told ahead of time in society? Are we repeating the past? Have we not learned what God has tried over and over to save us from, which is sin and the control of satan.

God in His wisdom has made a second plan in which only the righteous will get to receive and enjoy. God promise us the New Jerusalem, in which there will be no more sin, no more heartache, no more sickness, no more evil of any kind. A place of peace and worship where everyone worships God openly and gets to see God daily. A place where we get to live in Gods own capital of the universe and call it our home, call it a place of worship, for we will be able to live in Heaven—For forever and forever. That's the New Jerusalem so many have spoken about for centuries. Many believe it's here on Earth, but it clearly says in Revelation that God will come and remake Earth, remake His New Jerusalem once sin is gone forever and ever. Don't just take my word for it, or anybodies for the matter of fact, read your Bible yourself, and let God guide you onward homewards towards Heaven.

[Part 2 New Beginning]

As we carry on in this book, I will be sharing more of my thoughts, if you still are reading, thank you for taking the time to read my life travels thus far. Seeing into my minds battles, confusions and revelations. It is a little perhaps surprising, but I feel we all face such in different ways, so it's why I keep sharing on. In these pages is years of mind thoughts. From depressed days, to demonized drunken getting high days, to just childhood struggles.

We all have faced similar situations, and I hope and pray many of us won't ever have to live like this, that these pages can help guide you on correctly with God, giving you enough emotional drive behind the words to help you understand how confusion truly isn't what you want in your life. That what the world says is 'fun' are just allusions to a prison den. To deaden your potential to succeed with peace and clarity in mind. That long lasting peace only comes from God, so please listen. Please see past 'the moment' and see into the longevity of life.

Knowing you teens especially need to hear this, but slowly seeing, no matter how old you are, the second God comes into your life, we all are babies, so the content in here is for everyone, leaving may love be our core, our reason to keep on breathing.

Thank you.

A little insight for you all. Some perhaps may wonder how such a book could be written, for in some aspects it's very randomly put together. Many of my writings have been written over a long period of time. I didn't just sit down and begin writing. For a very long time, I was afraid to share my inner person struggles and thoughts, for I see them as sometimes a little deep, perhaps even crazy, but as you read and slowly connect all that is being said and done in the world, it all makes sense slowly, also understanding how life can torment you, it all smashes together. That as a child, as a teenager, yes the world can be very confusing, but now reflecting back, it makes perfect sense once God becomes a part of the story.

I'm just the expresser, expressing my life,

knowing also i'm just the messenger and i'm still growing on. We all are. Sharing is truly caring. Never be afraid to share your life story. The longer you carry on in God, the more spiritually you will become. That the battles you face are a daily reality; they come in all sort of ways. But when we have our 'crazy' moments it's us slowly figuring out life more, and God. Knowing we also have the devil in the equation of life just making it all that much more confusing and crazy. But the 'crazy' is simply us not understanding what's going on, so it's crazy in the moment, but once the storm passes and all settles and we reflect back with God, we will see that it all makes perfect sense. Having faith and trust is our key reminders to keep moving in life, with love & God leading us on.

— **Sir Knight Writes**—

My Mirrors Reflection

Inner Selfs Journal
Journey On
Part2
#LoveOn

[Our Songs]

Some walk on in their own song;
Which is right;
Their song belongs to them.
We forget to come out of that song to create new
songs with others in the mix of it.
Adding their own touch, their own piece, that
adds satisfaction,
While you add yours.
Yes, we walk on in our own song,
But we must know and understand how to
create new songs,
So we don't always walk alone,
Even if we know how to,
We never were made to,
For really, we are never alone,
Rather next to Jesus, and God, Leading us on.
Directing our song homeward heavenwards.
As we step on, sometimes we must ask these
questions, so we stay on track to keep the
marathon going.

[1, 2, 3 Steps]

You got to pick that chin up and look up-upward
Got to see the cowards and anything upside
down in your life and count backwards,
downwards, to ground zero-
To understand; seek clarity, finding conclusions.
Saying, "Hey maybe this means I'm at rock
bottom? But, what, no!

I won't give into this feeling,
This drilling of kill me!
Screw me!"
A feeling; Starting;
Counting back up upwards.
1, 2, 3 maybe I don't need you in my life right
now—4, 5, 6 neither you!
Either you help me positively now or you're
only pulling me downwards.
Looking around asking yourself what
surroundings you're taking part in?
7, 8, you're only around 1 out of 10 of the times;
Getting you further along your way downwards,
Giving you an award of fasts forwards my life to
death roll....
Slowly helping to take my heart apart.
I need a refill of God's loves dart to help repair
my mind and heart.
Now back, climbing up higher up to the
mountain top.
Sobriety bringing back real world feel reality;
Seeing the world's beauty starting to peek out
from death roll pews,
Seeing things in a new light-way view.
Down low blues starting to become real rockets
launching highway's excitement to the stars.
Basement levels starting to become elevators-
way to 100th floor doorways.
What's new someone asks? :)
I changed my life around and started to wear a

new happy face :) mask.
Started doing new tasks
Thanks for asking,
May we join hands in this and accomplish
something amazing?
Positivity becoming my new drug;
Wisdom becoming my best friend.
Trafficking in new hopes all the time man.
God comes knocking in too, helping me to scoop
up more love.
The more loved filled, the more possible I can do
those impossible duties people always said I
couldn't do.
Few years later approaching a friend,
"Hey, what's new with you?
Umm nothing man, I'm still hanging myself alive
Trying to survive—
Living off this smoke me up to get me high type
of suppose winner's type of vibes—!
Life's been riding me; —!
Grinding me, but I think I'm winning even
though my pocket says otherwise.
I think I'm wise,
But think partying each moment is the best way
onto life's golden gates highway.
"Hey man, I'm dropping low again, Wait a second
Let me get me something more quick......!"
Puff puff—gone! —
All better,
So at least I feel.

But my life mirrors tell differently."
Now ask yourself: "Can anyone relate?"
Sometimes we live in the moment too much.
Sometimes we forget life never stops, so why try
and slow it down? People do drugs, and all types
of addicting addictions etc. always trying to fill
this void, forgetting if you start living life and
doing more and more, life will become fulfilling.
Add love and God into it all and it becomes
complete more and more,
For understanding and wisdom becomes your
friend. Your best friend.

[Past Reflection]

Have those days where fire still comes out.
Somedays trapped by thoughts.
People think the past doesn't haunt.
Many don't understand just how far I have come
Where I was just a few years ago.
Forget about demons trying to attach back on.
Lately, put a lot of thought into such—
Think that doesn't put me into a mood of itself.
God, yes, He helps,
But what if I am attached onto my past too
much to let go?
For the clarity isn't there enough to fully let go?
What If I'm no saint in any standpoint and that
at any given moment could be a monster on fire
But thank God, God's love and care watches
over, protecting and guiding onwards.
Me some days allowing past demons to come
closer, wishing sometimes maybe I'll be happier

doing something where I feel I have a meaning
without having to fight them, knowing that truly
is impossible.
Forgetting some days, I already have a true
vision, a deeper soul purpose—
Being a lighthouse to all;
Shining God's love to others.
Other days feeling I'm doing something where I
see little to nothing happening,
Feel nothing about what I'm doing because I see
it as useless some days.
It's only God keeping me on track...Because me
myself can't.
Try to count my blessings, and trust me I got so
many.
But still alone by myself, not allowed to get close
to anyone.
For I cause trouble, cause pain, and I don't even
try.
It's like my job as a human is to cause pain,
By stating the facts.
They are just facts.
Facts set us free.
Cause little drops of love,
But more pain than love it would seem.
Perhaps I haven't found the balancing point yet
to switch it all around to more love than
anything else.
How can I say that's acceptable?
How can I say that's something to be justified?
It's not—

It's only like me frying myself alive with high-
fiving driving on monsters nearby laughing at
me.
Whispering in the air:
"I TOLD YOU SO!
ALL YOU EVER WILL BE IS EVIL!
A DEVIL OF YOUR OWN MAKING!
DON'T YOU DARE THINK YOU WILL BECOME SOMEONE
LOVABLE, BECAUSE REMEMBER YOU NEVER CAN BE!
UNDERSTAND HOMIE,
YOU SOME EVIL GENIUS WHO WITNESS YOURSELF AS
SOMEONE RIGHTEOUS,
WHICH IS JUST RIDICULOUS!"
So I must be.... maybe it's just me....my thoughts
bringing in more evil than good?
What if I took something and looked at it with
Gods own eyes?
Would I see it in a different light?
Maybe I would,
But with my own eyes,
I see connections of evil,
Why?
I hear something, and try to think good,
But hear within the good something bad,
Something ungodly,
So I dig-dig deeper into something negative.
Trying to switch to dig into something positive.
I got to ask,
Do I still have my head?
Or is it a half man, half demon head?
Stupid head I gotta be,
—Why does it feel like hell?

It should be all me & God in my head,
All listening upward to God.
Instead of—
Hearing voices saying,
"Welcome, welcome to hell son."
I got to pull out and say I got reason; I can't
commit treason.
Na, I could write all day,
And accomplish what?
That I'm a messed up screwed up kid still?
Still a sinner.
Still needing God more than ever.
Like isn't that what I'm getting at?
I'm still onto evil,
Without trying to be?
Maybe I'm judging myself,
But aren't you suppose to,
To help correct yourself?
Reflect to see your reflection?
Down low,
Up high,
Up-up sky high looking.
Drowned by garbage,
Down low by ages of pages of written scripted
dumpster monster garbage cans—
That keep creeping!
Wake up sweating,
Wondering if the past came back haunting.
Take a hate look evil note—
Trying to bring in a new love look note—
Double check what happened when chained by

an insane monster.
See people running;
See people running screaming,
Me looking out the window knowing I was some
snow widow monster spider.
An out eats you alive wind slider glider trigger
happy word tiger.
Rewind time in the wind and see me hiding:
Then popping out grinding.
My me, mind wind spinning when sinning and
penning be the ending.
Double digits be the hint; let it hit;
Do you get it?
No-
I don't think you do.
See me was a hide and seek you super glue on
cue all the time idiot.
Rotten garbage mind; capable of anything
monster.
Play with me and say with me hello; gets it;
Hell-O.
A hell hole made played and said;
So see once upon a day I took a holy book and
did something unfavorable, unforgivable,
So double glued to hell I be.
See I feel holy some days,
Then other days, feel back to a black hole
trapped in abysses so dark nobody can even
hear me.
Witness hisses and kisses,
Wishing, missing me, messing with me,

Me playing a peek-a-boo who are you game face
Saying amazing grace be my happy face while
holding my golden made God's Word mace.
Laced up shoes causing people to be needing
tissues.
Pull people's real issues out and make them feel
like nothing is excused.
For it never was for me,
Forgetting love should be the filler, so it can be
excused.
Rescue me while I play recess while texting my
ex-saying what happened?
Did you help cause this mess, I don't know,
But I think not.
I rot,
Was taught to be a rotten forgotten begotten son
of a son,
By a demon whispering.
So, is this said for fun, or am I being for real —
you feel me?
I think not,
Cause I don't even feel me some days;
Maybe I'm a robot!
My fist out busting something down quick so it
won't be missed.
I missed my chance,
I danced along the idea maybe I could be saved,
And I can be,
But in this,
I feel satan still out attacking, coming with axes
asking:

"Why you still here doing nothing holy?
Boy, you out trying, aren't you?
No boy—!
Aren't you trying man—!
I KNOW YOU ARE.
But kid,
Who do you kid,
When you ask how I am not a saint?
You a satan kid still: and you know it, Don't you-
No, you don't know it,
But think about it,
Say it—!
Just say it!"
||
No—!
NEVER!
I won't come back fighting you with words
anymore,
Because I found the Lord and closed this door,
But I know I invite you back by thinking about
this hiss miss me kiss you wishing playing
wheel steel feel —made walls — lions dens walls;
Fire proof— now you trying to put me back into
denial.
I taught nothing to nobody about this; or did I?
It's hard to see any of it clearly anymore.
It's just old pasted files that come rushing in
whenever they desire.
Why some ask—
I don't know why?
Maybe it's judgment day, and I'm being judged.

Double, triple, judged.
Put on a magic rug on a treadmill running along
seeing flashbacks of everything.
See me laughing,
Having fun,
Not thinking about anything important really,
Feeling this warmth from shots,
Seeing demons running around next to me,
And me somehow loving it,
It's all coming together into a mixing wheel,
Spinning on in my mind reminding me at least I
would feel something while under the influence.
See me back off the influence—
Me crawling waddling on in hallways pacing
uptight out ready to yell at anyone—!
To now,
Me sober out feeling little to nothing but shallow
emotions most days to some days getting hit
hard with emotions of the past...
See out in the future and feel this helpless feel
that nothing can stop what's to come,
So sharing all so hopefully someone can take the
positive out of these past dark shared
reflections.
See me as an useful instrument,
Feel God nearby,
Feel evil around all the time,
Seeing it's all a focus issue.
Seeing I can't think about the past much longer.
Feel peace within the mixture of feelings and it's
beginning not to be a feeling anymore,

But a reality form of boredom.
Hear a message saying you can't trust feelings,
And I know that,
But it's human nature to feel something,
To feel, to have a reason for taking your next
breath.
Put reason and logic behind everything,
Though some days I drop that and could care
less about my soul's salvation,
So it would seem,
But deep down care to the utmost.
Because it's whenever I do something evil, I feel
again.
Then feel regret deeply.
When I do kind deeds,
I feel amazing, and stay feeling so until it's
realities settle.
I also feel again,
But you can't do kind deeds all the time while
you're by yourself.
You can't always be helping,
You got to make a living,
Making a job duty come into reality.
Got to entertain yourself somehow, but how do
you wonder onto.
Think heavenly and feel good about it,
Then come back down to earth and have this
moment of wanting to do something so
remarkable that you will become unstoppable
with a message to save people—
Then you look back in the mirror and see you

can't even save yourself from your nightmare of
a nutcase mind, Feeling it's a trapped mind.
Hear God saying He can save you,
He can give you clarity,
Understanding.
And you believe Him,
But then don't—
See Him enough to believe after awhile—
You go do some more evil after a while and see
yourself as a monster.
Look back at God and start to wonder if you're
playing games again?
Hear warning after warning—
Hey boy you about to go sinning again,
And it stops you for a while,
But then after a while,
You're like whatever,
I know if I do this or that,
I'll feel a little better,
So go on you do and have your fun, and then
look back and say to God I sinned,
Already knowing you did beforehand, Making
the sin premeditated sin.
Making it almost unforgivable.
Making hell sound its door open a little bit more.
You looking at yourself saying,
"Well I didn't go get drunk;
I didn't go get high;
I didn't do nothing as bad as I used to do.
So is it worthy of hell?"
For a while daily praying to God to have a

purpose,
Then after a while don't even bother to pray
anymore,
Because it's like praying to a wall.
Saying,
"Well If I fall is it my fault?"
But of course it is.
You can't go blaming God for anything.
At the end of the day it's all you doing what you
do.
God cares,
You know He cares,
But you also know He knows all—
For God knows all, guides all, and knows when
you truly will be ready to take on more
responsibility and when you need more time to
fully understand the past, and present, so you
can carry on forward with a sane mind.
Echoing all and any are welcome into heaven if
they follow God with all their understanding
and hearts.
After a while you start to go a little crazy by
thinking too much.
I swear,
Each day you begin to write,
You go a little bit deeper into it all.
Thinking once you're done and reread
everything you will say,
Maybe I'm not crazy—
Finding your saner than sane.
Just mind racing,

Saying only the well comprehensive will fully connect and understand.
But in reality you're just a little bit more spiritual than most people.
Or maybe I'm to proud of myself and see it as I want to see it as.
But look at it that way for a long while and say no, it is just what it is.
See some days I feel I could be someone so important,
Then some days where I'm put back into my place, and see myself as nothing, I just get less and less emotional about things.
Then have to come back in yelling at myself, telling myself,
"Hey boy it won't kill you to show some emotions."
You can't be hiding all your emotions inside you all the time, you best come out smiling even though it's a lie, though is it?
You feel happy when you smile, but on top of that feel sad still,
But why?
Feel something that after a while, you can't even say you feeling anything but everything, but then are you even feeling or are you just at an emotional level of unknown that you can say you feeling nothing?
For you really feel it all too much to put an understanding to it.
You keep carrying on in your minds spinning

wheel ,wondering why you do so, besides
knowing if you write it down, it can least be said,
and done with, filed down, so your future self
can reread and see just how much growth has
been done.
Thanking God now, and ahead a time for being
so understanding and loving.
Hoping and praying whoever reads this can
understand my past confused me.
But also relate even their own life related
thoughts some days to this.

| | | | | | | | | | |

As we grow older and mature, we all face
questions. Sometimes the questions are deeper
than others, but either way, we all ask these
questions. As you read on, you will soon learn
about my past in a more direct story way,
which will allow you to understand me much
better. Yes, in my last book I mention about it a
lot, for it is my reflection book, but now I want
you to fully understand in a broader way.

[Blessings]

Ever seen something that's hard to explain?
Makes your brain and heart almost feel this
pain—
You see something that is so simple and know of
things that are so complicated.
That when you try to step into the simplest form
of what you see,
It puts you somewhere else in a different time
almost.

Most people think if you could have this and that,
Life would be complete.
Forgetting the simple roots of life, that they aren't ever truly living,
But always working for something they may never achieve.
If you think on a simpler note and live to a simpler beat,
Life will be peaceful.
It's when you reach out for so many things all at once,
That life starts to become a burden,
A stress killer, and slowly starts to ruin your enjoyment in life.

Keynote reminders

Friends, family, basic needs, God and a place that's peaceful is all you need to be happy.
After that,
Count everything else as added on blessings.
We all are given different pathways to walk and lead.
Within each pathway,
Choices are given,
You choose so much of your outcome.
Seek into the past,
Even if it's dark,
Learn the lessons,
Cherish the good times,
Grow on,
Love,

For out of love,
All good things come.
For God is love.
Also, so you can slowly become more loving.

[Cards Giveth]

It's been hard,
It's been rough,
But it's never enough.
I played life's long hard cards;
I'm talking lawn yard driven cards.
What do I mean?
I am saying I been through so much you can
ride on its pages.
Been back down trapped into hellish ages.
Wishing I had a wishing wheel for a while.
But was in denial.
Saw destiny coming into reality talking.
I close my eyes and see charmed talked marked
chalk lines within the lines spinning.
Wonder if somedays I'm still winning?
Know somedays I'm still sinning.
Thinking, placing down the inking.
Wearing out hot pink colors of life and lighting it
off.
Been in midnight conditions without AC
temperatures.
Hell heat fire heated sweating thinking getting
high.
Seeing pretty red filled colors of pictures.
Looking up; holding up my head high and saying
oh my—

I say oh my, why oh why can't I die?
Picture red; picture red blue pink and think.
Think-think thinking if I fall down off a cliff will
I be better off?
About to jump, then I go off—
Off at how off I am with my thinking.
I come back spinning and having winning on in
my mind going calling upon evil.
"Wait, why evil?"
It's what I taught myself.
Now taught myself to call to God—Calling God
daily.
Facing past demons and God daily.
Devil coming calling saying,
"If you falling just give me a calling and I'll stop
the bawling.
I'll stop your crawling.
Shh, baby boy....so shy you baby boy.
You a yo-yo and a play toy."
Oh heck no, I'm coming running drumming a
humming and saying I'm nobody dumbing.
No zombified out drinking.
Devil came in whispering in—
"Okay okay, play a note that's musical."
You a general.
You for real?
Digging deep into the cold gone gold mind.
See in my mind and you see Einstein.
Devil back:
"But baby lets' rewind, come back into time.
You said you wanted something defined and

divine.
You can be all mine if you give me your time.
It won't cost you a dime.
I promise double triple multiplied by lies.
Trust me, look into my eyes, please.
I'm not saying I'm Jesus, but I'm saying I'm
jealous.
See I'm not out to overcome nothing.
I'm just trying to say something.
You out wanting marvelous wonders and
something wonderful—"
No way devil, I'm not full of foolishness.
I'm full of awesomeness.
God guided.
You devil like:
"Watch this diss miss track dismiss a miss a hiss
—hiss kiss.
Wish I swish—; a dish —
Pitch with a pitch fork horn throwing."
De see devil—
You try and wish me evil, but no—
God wishes me good.
I'm in a good mood saying I'm fired up with jet
fuel lighting, Gods.
The fact of the matter is I'm the fool for even
talking to you to begin with.
Some days feeling:
Na I'm just a tool used to be cool whispers in—
Power drill out drilling thinking which killing
machine descriptive word I'll use next.
Word fiddling,

Building a word building that will
Bust through the ceilings.
Once it's done.
| | | | | | | | |
We all have been through so much in life. Have
so many good stories to tell, just as we do bad
ones. Good and evil is very real. Choose to listen
to the positive in all, and if you hear the
negative, wonder why, but learn not to listen to
that side usually, for it doesn't matter how bad
something is, there can always be a positive
outlook to it, if you allow yourself to see it.

[By & By]

By and by we glide through life seeing and
hearing strange things.
Time and time each ride giving us new life—
Changing us, allowing us a chance to spring new
wings to see what once was hidden.
Looking through the window glass seeing the
connections easier and more clearly now.
The fact of the matter is, the puzzle is still being
connected more and more.
The surprises are still coming springing in all
the time, letting its beauty ring on telling me
there's still so much more gliding to do, that life
can never get boring unless we make it so.
Holding out hope that I find when I look out and
still see nature still going on, lively as ever.
Asking God why I can't believe more?
Can't let go now, not after all I been through.
Looking through the eyes window seeing other

eye windows looking back at me—
Wondering if they see right through me or see
someone else's reflection?
Asking for correction, seeing optical neglecting.
Or perhaps that's me rejecting correction that I
don't see it all clearly.
Merely looking for something to appear, but
think maybe that's not possible.
See something impossible, and question rather
if it can be possible.
Each day I go moving on thinking on along the
lines of past done mind thought moments.
Feeling pain sometimes; living in the moment,
Going back and forth—
Dodging demons along the way—Thinking how I
could sway away from that way and that way to
create my new song in God?
Seeing new days coming, drum line humming,
me maybe getting dumber, but thumbs up I say
and go on moving that dumber moment into a
number one moment.
Humming hum-tee-dum love on along the way,
as I do life like a bumblebee.
See me the happiest when I'm feeling alive.
Survive, survive, survive on—
Whispers on in my mind—
Saying, "You'll never die; just keep your eyes on
God."
Giving life a high five.
Going taking a dive in my mind and seeing
which side comes up once coming back up.

Maybe all be upside down or sideways.
But each day,
I'm going moving on thinking how can I make
life a little bit better?
How can I make the world better?

||

As you move on in life, it's beautiful to stop and
see the beauty that life has to give, but
sometimes the things life can give are deceiving.
So be careful, try to put understanding and
reasoning into your decision making.
Following morals and the Ten Commandments.
For it allows you to keep walking on straight.
As we try to keep a positive mindset; a positive
outlook, we sometimes have to try harder than
other days.
Some days, some months and even years are
harder than others. But if we choose to count
our blessings, our gifts, our lives; we start to see
perhaps maybe we aren't as bad off as we
thought we were.

[Roses?]

Roses, yes roses show us different beauty.
They show us under its flowers of beauty there
still can be thorns.
They blow in a variety of color and form.
Roses flowing out calling out choosing you.
Are you a red and violet one with glamorous
beauty or a blue and grey one with more thorns
of horns that cause merely misery than flowers
of love from above?

Roses, yes roses tell us so much more than what is simply seen, it's remarkable.
As you walk by, your reflection is cast out onto others leaving a pedal of love or a thorn of sorrow; so tomorrow which rose do you choose to be?

During the mist of good times, it's easy to show love, to show happiness, to walk the straight line, but when those darker times come, we are tested, we are put to our max. I'm still learning to control my emotions fully, for as you have read, my younger self wasn't, my mind raced on, and on to places that I never had to dwell in, but I allowed myself to by not controlling my emotions, leaving storms to develop on in my mind.
Leaving some days even still for anxiety to develop.
I'm sure you can relate of facing days where you argue between rather you're doing good or bad. Rather what you have done really matters.
We all do it, but why?
Usually because we are seeking for clarity; seeking to learn more, to simply just understand. When we don't know the answer, this is when anxiety can come in. For our minds starts doing half circles, and keep doing so trying to understand. Many times, this allows problems to happen that never would of if we just simply would of given it to God and had Him

worry about it and moved our focus onto something we can truly do in the moment. Next time life gives you troubles, pause and pray, pray that God will calm you down, and tell Him to worry about it, and I promise you, you will become more peaceful and since you are going to God, He will bless you with the wisdom you need to carry on in life. Remember His time and our time are different, so do not become impatient, rather learn to just focus on other things in life that you can, and know God hears you all the time, have faith, He always knows best. #LoveOn

[Storms]

I got storms coming when I coming with my thinking.
But is it mine or my inter most mist?
I got my fist out ready to risk it!
But no I mid kid!
You a kid — I a kid!
Why should I die for that?
I don't know, but you do?
You follow me for some odd reason.
What you waiting for me to commit some old treason?
Ready to go and be my sons of sons?
What lies of lies just said.
Why oh why let me get to your head?
I just said something, possibly me making it make believe like Sony.
Yeah yeah Sir Knight coming over kidding

bidding a hidden message.
Coming over under wondering why under under
I be some space odd man wondering on n' on n'
on to the den dawn.
Hint hint: whoa star light of the morning dawn
dawn dawn.
Yeah not me, but the one who controls so many
evil foes.
Who gotta come and say enny-meeny-miny-
moe! I'm no rhino but maybe a tornado.
Started in Orlando and drove my Volvo till
death. Yeah been to those depths but now I got
swept down till I wilted and wept.
I felt what was felt cause I dealt it.
But now hate it!
So quite it investigators gators!
Don't you dare try and make me some maker.
Black black dark clouds could form if I allowed
evil to control.
Me and evil could be a squeal qual to soar over
the oceans as eagles.
Many don't see that as possible, but possible it is
easily.
But I choose to neglect it for it rejected me when
I want it, but now I changed my inter most mist
school scholarship n' battleship subject to super
sub development-ship in places no space ship
could ever dip its wings into.
For in its place all is calm.
Happiness is at it's purest.
Angels sing of it's heavenly psalms.

Its place is filled with holiness.
Moodiness, cruelness, sadness, meanness is
meaningless for it doesn't reach into it's
atmosphere, neither does fear or a tear from
evilness for sinlessness is there and sin it selfish
self is finished, diminished for those who are
vicarious.
So carry on;
Fight on;
Jesus has your back.

[Jumping]

We jump into life hopping.
We bounce back up and down like a basketball.
We think big and dream even bigger.
We fall sometimes while other times blow are
own minds completely away.
Life's an adventure.
It's a painting and your painting your own
picture.
What colors will you put onto your master
piece?
What impact will your master piece show?
What secrets will be secretly placed?
What love will be honored and reflected back at
you the painter.
Will you be the hater or the forgiver,
Taking and painting it out?
I choose to be the lover, the fighter of higher
powers,
God ready hand steady;
Stating the stated known, so the unknown can

slowly become known.
Growing the small seeds into huge large
unstoppable ones.
Ask the little questions so the big ones aren't
confusing, they are rather sensible.
You as the painter have to ask these questions.
Then the picture you paint as the painter will
have depth and curves.
Each word said, asked, has meaning.
Each stroke of your paint brush is you pushing
on in life.
What will you push on for?
What strokes will you stroke onto your master
piece?
What will your verse say?
How will you play it?
Will you love it?
For you will have to live in it.
Live in love.
For love is where happiness is at.

[Sky Lines]

Sky blue.
Yellow me down dude blue.
Soon snow shall come changing things.
Playing with super glue because I'm attracted to
too many horrible things for earth is sickening
with wickedness.
Unchanged so it seems.
Light beams swinging in shining.
Smiling, mining time, divined things of kings.
Thought of as nothing.

Thought of by myself as everything, but maybe
that's me being to prideful.
Gotta believe in something though like God.
Hold strong to it all or else take a fall.
Never take a fall for forever though.
Go through any endeavor climbing up out of the
hellish elevator into Gods throne begging for
forgiveness, for understanding, for more love.
Over thrown evil saying I played the game, and
was changed, and changed again and again till I
grin now at such sought out fame of devilish lies
Was played as a robot in an evil mans game.
Framed as a perfect picture monster — a
dumpster hipster devil minister of falseness.
Now a nobody for if nobody I gotta be,
I will be as long as I do no evil no more.
I explore my mind and find pass memories that
shake me down.
I dig into my inter-most mind and find new
surprises of good riches of unforetold glory
given to me by God.
Some days I am faceless, but inside my mind is
spinning so fast falling in love with the idea of
peace that lays out there in Heaven.
I count seven times seven times seven be the
amount of times I shall think upon such, and
another seventy more times till infinity.
I try to be a friend to any in till then.
A caring loving person to any foreign city that's
still crying for help;
Helping them out of their lions den.

A help to those who don't appear to be so pretty in the inside.

A higher standing guy who try's to only be as strong as stone so any alone can have a shield, a mentor, and leader if need be.

I am weak, but I can become strong if God sees fit.

Perfect picture beauty I seek.

Ask me if I care about the meek, and I speak and say surely I must, because I care for all.

Again throw your problems onto me and I'll only try to up lift and help, seeking my help from God, leaving so can you.

If I got to be an air vent for you, I will be so also so you can breathe and live.

If I have to come swinging in colors as a rainbow to up lift your day, I will because your hurt was felt.

I only try to be the best I can.

The man I was suppose to always be, so I stand with an open hand.

A person of Gods own image.

All of us can shine off Gods character; for we our His children written down in His pages.

His highest delight throughout the ages.

His beloved soon Angels.

So change on to perfection we must try thrusting onward, knowing as long as progress is happening we are doing something right.

Rusting out the old me to change me into the new me that God sees fit.

Busting out the garbage and chasing that away,
changing that into real true freedom because
I'm a bee who is free.
I'm me,
Believe me,
Breathe,
Relax,
Life can only get so bad before it starts to get
better.
Throw yourself at God, for He is always there,
always for you, and will always be loving and
kind to you.

[Life]

The more I live, the more I understand slowing
things down doesn't harm you.
Being patience doesn't prevent you from
anything, but helps you to fully see more.
Time is precious, but sometimes time is what
needs to take place so when you do go do
something in life, it has meaning,
Has purpose,
Has a deeper motive behind it, because it's
carefully thought after, and thus truly genuine
and authentic. So many precious moments have
been lost,
Haven't been fully made,
Because of rushing things.
You wish you said this, wish you could have
done that, wish you saw it differently......well
why not do that? Sometimes a little longer for
something is what makes something golden.

Makes it forever memorable.

[Eyes Opened]

As you open your eyes, you never know what
you may see next.
You may see a child out looking for their
parents.
Maybe a thief out ready to take something.
Possible a baby duck following its mother in a
beautiful pound surrounded by trees and bushes
and flowers eating some food about ready to go
and rest....
Maybe a man on a roof top half hanging off it
trying to attach a gutter; you wondering if he
has spider gens.
Maybe a cloud and within that cloud you see a
familiar face.
Maybe something so amazing you can't even
begin to explain it because your brain isn't
knowing yet how to.
Maybe a nest filled with baby birds reaching out
their long neck like mouths to get fed.
Maybe a hand crafted basket that's beautiful
because detail and passion was thrown into it.
Whatever you may see, look at it as though it
was the first time seeing it, because then new
beauty will be seen, new lessons will be learned,
and new connections and parallels between
different things will be made, but most
importantly, life will never get old then.

[Moments]

In one moment we can stand or fall.
In one minute we can hold out our hand or
stand pridefully tall.
In one argument we can walk away and let
things calm down or cause unforgettable chaos.
The balance of control is in you if you allow time
and patience to take it place.
The peace is always in your soul if you allow God
to take control.
The ability to bring reality into perfect harmony
isn't always possible unless you connect into the
source Who controls it all, God.
Life is a mess, is a world-spin of sin within a
series of unstoppable events awaiting to
happen.
Beauty lays out there among the sight of a
creeping beast wanting to unleash its wrath and
bring all and any down its pathway.
The question is this: will you let the negative of
this world control you; or will you look onward
out of this world to heaven— having your insight
be transformed into something that only sees
glowing beauty and hope for humanity; aligning
your eyes upon Jesus as your compass, so the
past can be the past and the future can be the
future; having an incomparable picture of
perfect love, for all you feel for others is love,
because God is love, and He is your all so you
can never fall, but stand tall as a lighthouse for
righteousness.

Next Thought

Have you simply just looked up and admired the beauty that lies in the skies?
Have you opened your eyes to take in the moment of the passing times that have all types of wonders within them?
Do you let life get the best of you or do you allow life to pause and let things slow down, so each and every moment you can see something precious and beautiful?
Sometimes slowing life down only helps you enjoy it.
Because you are getting to remember it, enjoying it's simpleness.
Remembering what's most important in this life.
Looking through the window glass towards Jesus.
Keeping His light as your compass.
Keeping your heart open for Him to dwell in.
Smiling through it all.
Because He is your all.

Next Thought

Feeling life saying something.
Actions telling nothing.
Digging till clarity is sought and found.
Home bound calling smelling flowers.
Seeing the hidden objects in the hour glass.
First class passes laughing all awhile.
Smiling faces appearing from alien followers.
First comers coming saying wait why can't I be last?
Blast loaded off to unearthly home bound

unimaginable places.
Palaces of golden olden unfolded untold
opportunities creeping out hollering, yelling,
telling, I told you so.
Hold out my hand one last time asking why can't
I be likable?
Why am I some intolerable being looking as good
as marble appearing as though an unstoppable
substance.
Which subject am I even referring to many be
thinking.
Asking why I place down in the ink what I do?
Some wonder is he thinking or linking some
pinky written thinking.
Not understanding which type of thinking error
once occurring.
Not understanding, I'm just the messenger,
Sometimes the message isn't for me or you, but
for him and her; they will understand, perhaps
one day so will we.
Some wondering if he is trying to be accepted or
if he rejects acceptance and appearance
anymore.
Perhaps peering through looming looking
glasses.
Seeing things in different light compare to
many, that at the end of it, I'm so caught up in
its new lights that I think not what others will
see me as, but as what will God and me see
myself as in ten years.
Appearing looking into the future mirror and

seeing a beautiful wife, life, lived and gave.
Family roses appearing.
Houses showing love, life, beauty,
Remembering peace, honor;
Giving, severing, helping, bettering, together
bettering,
Flying in the motto song of loves forever love
song.
Over what people think of me,
So setting myself free,
and being me.

[Memory Lane]

I can walk down memory lane and learn nothing
or choose to learn a lot.
Been to hell and back.
Chose a painful experience at first.
But my second and third verse doesn't have to
be so because I found God, so next page.
I choose to step into different shoes:
Changing and fixing any past mislead misfired
committed acts.
Axing and chopping them until they are old past
done facts.
Never giving a chance to go back.
Forever giving love back to set back evil.
Climbing any endeavor and double triple looking
forward at Bible verses before I mingle.
Fly now with Angles and Gods Eagles.
Dekle be my last name.
Family crest name means number one, so I say
let me be last so only then can I appreciate being

number one after everyone else gets there first.
I guess you can say I adore and admire others,
Get inspired by seeing others enact their
enacted gifts of life that they were bestowed,
enquired, practiced, made, thus wired and
created to be, so I respect all who seek to try, to
better.
I'm a past down blood line knight, meaning I
fight standing up to all haters and demons.
You ask me what's next: I say I don't know, I'm
only a person giving a message.
The rest is for the Doctor of all ages, aka Jesus
Christ to tell what happens next.
I wish all could know Him and have that close
relationship.
For only then can true peace and love be
attained.
Next Thought
Try to better.
Try changing things for the better.
Go forth putting others before self, bringing joy
to all for only then will things get better.
Humbleness has its power that many never
truly learn to appreciate.

[Created]

Look at your fingertips, and see just how
complicated they are and how everyone's are
different.
Now look at how small, yet important they are.
How they have such a functionality to your
everyday lives.

Now tell me you're not blessed, that thought and
detail wasn't put into it, into you, that we just
didn't happened to involve into such beings
having these senses of touch and feelings;
Having complex inter narrow thinking and
individual DNA structures,
Saying who you just are.
Wild isn't it?
That God made you,
You.
Be you.
Let love be you.
Next Thought
You ever ask yourself, why does love have to be
so powerful?
How can it blind us and control us so easily?
Is it our compassionate character that steps in
and endures our downfalls?
Allowing others to hold us on even longer,
grounding our self's to each other just a little bit
more, because we start to know what's
acceptable and what is simply pushing it to the
limit of someone's emotions.
What if you put others first naturally, how then
would the outcome be for you as you approach
someone else? Lowering yourself and trying to
understand them before reacting.
Leaving all your actions having a second
reflection before enacting.
So more time to make the best choices can
happen.

Leaving sound judgment, yours.
Beautiful once you think about it some more.

[Waking]

You wake me asking:
Why you still living?
I reply back saying I don't know,
I should be long gone by now.
Somehow mighty wings stay maintaining me
keeping me motivated.
Me keeping God in mind all the time trying to
stay as divine as possible.
Rewinding time in my mind tracking back wild
things, finding timing and dividing life equations
equipped with more questions turning them into
understandables;
Keep adding new words to the dictionary;
Questioning the hesitations, still covering,
hovering life's all.
Wonder why we still here in this messed up
world yet anyways?
How many more got to go down in history as the
fallen, as the saved;
The precious saints?
What would it take for a deflated world to be
brought back into airs circulation;
Flying back into orbit correctly on target to its
home ground designed destiny heaven;
Heaven being crowned in glorious promises of
new lands to come, new realities to be lived,
New places to travel, to explore, to adore it all—
Our foundational homes destination Heaven—

paradise;
Where only:
God, Family, Friends are at;
With no pain, sorrows, hardships, evil, nor
harmful things imaginable shall be there;
Equaling final settlement for ever lasting
happiness in love,
In God.

[Awaken]

A billion more fallen asleep to be awaken with
another tornado giving no mercy for another
tomorrow.
Sin follows sin,
Good follows good,
It's really that simple.
Be the good,
The love.
Do you go base on your guts feelings or over
your fears stopping you from bringing in the
clear visions of what
true reality is:
Which is love:
Peace,
God
Grace,
Family,
Harmony,
Morals,
Forgiveness,
Workmanship,
Fellowship,

Leadership,
Gods Laws;
Forever Lasting Happiness.
Endless knowledge,
Adventure, Creations,
Ideas to yet be heard of.
A place love lives on all the time,
Shining its beautiful light, radiating the skies
with Gods grace, love, kindness, mercy,
forgiveness, with oneness, that life will never
grow old or boring at all.
Only more and more fulfilling with
Love & Peace Living On Forever;
Love On knowing that those make life truly
worth living for.

[Choices]

You can't base decisions off feelings.
You can't touch rock bottom unless you truly
believe there's no more hope left.
You can't chase after something or someone
who doesn't want chasing after forever,
For all you will get is this hurt disappointing
feeling.
You can say whatever you want, but that doesn't
mean you will or can do whatever you want.
Life's somewhat a living awaking dream,
You can vision it as one so tackling the
impossible can become possible.
This life is meaningless unless you find love to
hold on to.
Passion and love and reason have to go into

your decisions for true devolution to come into
play to revolutionize your eyes and give you a
worthy end goal prize, that's seen as your
precious gold.
Each passion gives you something to hold,
meaning rock bottom is never an option.
Each dear soul to you,
Gives a more accurate detail reason to have
compassion for others.
Whatever you say, you should do.
Life has no limitations if you go after your
dreams.
Love is the key to the universe,
Meaning it's awfully important.
Each verse and line said only allows you to leave
a mark for others to benefit from.
What has your eyes seen that you find import?
What does your verse say to the universe,
To us?
Let it say,
Love,
Love Forever On

[Longing On]

The longing to hold something precious.
The bogging and jogging to find that gold that's
marvelous.
The dodging and gliding through hidden old past
cobwebs to see something glorious.
The lonely ride of the sea night sailor whispers
taunting serious hisses of missed wishes.
The trapped underground gold miners mind

gone off in ditches and doneness wrenches.
The twisted told lies leading to dead laid
trenches without reward of pay, so away with
him and on way with a new.
The delayed end for we don't dare call it a day,
unless we can say we gave it our all.
Our her-ray yay yeah we tried.
The last shouted out prayer to ask God for
forgiveness as we witness decay.
Sand, dirt, dust and clay is all that we are once
we our laid to rest.
Hurt filled hearts lost and confused, senseless to
the mess, so we run around and play.
The within known fact that taunts everyone
though: maybe it truly is the end.
The longing for something though will always
whispers on and on till will, soul and heart find
its precious marvelous glorious golden home.
Until that day we fiddle and build and riddle
along our way reaching out to our brothers and
sisters;
Calling to come home,
Because we wouldn't want to live another day
without them present with us,
Living, surviving thriving on into eternity with
us.
For we only think on an enteral basis, leaving
us with a never ending, but a journey that truly
is incredible.
Let's set aside our differences and see what we
can see.

I look into a mirror and see myself and some
days see this monster, other days I look and see
this prince on fire.
And some days this nightmare of a man hanging
on to nothing, but I continue on anyways.
Mind in zone on being the higher being and kind
fellow knight staying as original as possible.
Keeping a hold of the deep roots of putting
others first;
God, family, friends is all that matters,
Though some days I see that as impossible.
Loneliness of the loneliness,
Taunted by demons,
Comforted by angels.
So I try to find anything that's dissolvable,
becoming doable and redo-able, taking the
trash, the hurt, the pain, and turning it into
pure gold, submitting the committed and
commenting on all that life lets me fall upon.
Praying ahead of time,
As the words fall,
They fall to those who need it most.
#LoveOn

[Moments Pass]

Moments pass,
Opportunities within those life throbbing
dashes.
Heads come together and laugh and heads
smash.
Rash detentions coming moving in fast creating
undoable realities.

Sentimental mentalities grove in its own habits.
This must have its poison within controlling.
Emotions may be its name?
Life's rolling all along.
Moments pass, will yours matter or be
pointless?
Be the sweetness,
The love of goodness.

[Our Beauty]

Some question what beauty is.
Some wonder what it is to be real.
Some wonder on to what others think about
them.
Some look only at appearance as true beauty.
Some think being real is living doing everything
humanly possible that's satisfying as being real.
Let's dive into this equation and see what can be
found.
If you look at someone you see outwardly a lot.
But from the viewer, all they see is appearance.
From that they can tell simple basic information
about the person.
If they are skinny, fat, sexy, adorable, cute,
beautiful, scary, scatter brained, mental,
gorgeous, etc.
They can also tell rather if they care about how
they look, if they keep up with themselves, if
they try to hard to appear as someone they are
not, if fitness and health matters to them, if
fashion is important and more or less who they
try to stand for, which sometimes can be so

false, but usually is pretty true.
The viewer also can begin to read facial
expressions which begins to let them slowly
start to go dive into the persons being and
character.
From that they begin to see what's real inside.
See more light from them.
Once conversation begins to happen and
exchanging of information takes place; more
emotional actions and vibes are released.
From such a liking or disliking or non-caring-
ness starts to form within each person.
If relative ideas, thoughts and likings are found;
instantly a deeper relationship of a friendship is
grounded and established.
Allowing thus for a more opened expression of
self to be opened freely without worrying what
the other will think because already the
beginning stages of trust are rooting.
As they dive into each other's minds further, the
more and more likings are found; disliking's,
and connections are made, allowing for a
stronger understanding of one another, and
hopefully a deeper respect for one another is
developed. Sometimes a separation from not
having that respect, or same aspect of view etc.
can develop too, leaving devision to happen.
As all this is taking place, the persons
appearance starts to change for the viewer
because now they are not just viewing and only
seeing the outside but also connecting the

outside and inside into one focal view point,
giving the viewer finally a conclusion of who
that person is, as in for an example:
By connecting bitterness, awesomeness,
sexiness, funniness, seriousness, adorable,
intelligence, thoughtfulness, daringness, caring,
adventurous, cunningness, etc! All into a name,
a person is made, thus truly you are made real,
for you are not shallow, are not perfect, but are
human, a being who thrives on as someone
trying to live life and shine off who you are, and
trying to become; creating your name as not
just a name, but a name with hundreds of words
backing that name that makes you
irreplaceable.
Sorry perhaps over thinking it, but I don't believe that is ever
possible:}
Next Thought
We truly are incredible in more ways than we
give ourselves credit at times.
With our stunning ideas, dreams, passions; we
have more to us than we even know.
For with such ideas, it shows just how much
unknown wonders lay within us.
For connecting, making anything into
something it is exercising our minds;
Our souls are beautiful, are beyond gorgeous,
our hearts are hearts of lions, tigers, queens,
and kings. Compassionate passion lays within
us all, sometimes we just have to go and try
hard to find it; battle through it; learning,
growing, becoming, maintaining, loving,

holding, cherishing—; once these truly are
found; compassion and passion guides us, giving
us unimaginable emotions, giving us life to feel
for others on a level that is very real.
A sense of knowing any type of pain and
heartbreak gives us advantage over many, for
we know what pain can do and cause.
So compassion we have, learning to love;
To give,
Giving growth inside our hearts.
Being kind, patient; lets us become more
sympathetic.
The wanting to be wanted gives us a loneliness
that we wish could be filled.
The wanting-ness to be held and comforted tells
us we are very human, and that once we find
someone to love us, we won't ever let them go.
Our smiles are true power, so smile often. Let
the love from within us shine out, we have
mountain loads of love left in us from God, and
God helps us to truly be a positive person.
We are capable to forgive, it is hard at times, but
love from God helps us.
Our dreams in life will all be different, but put
God first and never be last.
Put love into whatever you do, and I promise
success will be your end result for everyone is
attracted to love.
God loves a person who cherishes love, for love
is sounded throughout the universe, meaning
our actions of love are sounded straight into

heaven bringing Gods loads of joyful tears.
The fighter side in us is strong.
The determination to not give up is so also.
Once all is said and done, we're not just
stunning, but beautifully gorgeous by being
simply us.
So be yourself always,
But you.
The ability in us to keep growing on into more
and more of a person of character is truly there,
truly possible, just believe you can achieve
whatever you seek after to achieve.
Be willing to simply listen to people, the power
in that is beyond awesome.
We all are teachable, trainable and well capable
of anything we set our minds to.
#LoveOn

[Stage]

We stage something,
But what?
We age,
But why?
We say sayings and state things,
But don't move.
I try, you try.
You cry, I cry.
I love, you love.
You do you, I do me.
How are you, why so blue?
Some question if I do something will it make a
difference or if I do what you do will it then

matter more, following in after the norm of ideal
normal, so to fit in.
Formal small horns now appear as little thorns.
While big mainstream steam engine devil horns
appear as magical and habitual and natural, so
we accept anything willingly, killing any moral
mentality left and then aski why is there such
crime and hate in the world when we have
allowed our own minds to be so blind sided.
Bidden in a hidden trap period of prideful living.
Saying only the brave survive to stay another
day.
People in charge saying:
"But it's not us; we didn't do this.
We didn't invite this mess.
We didn't witness us as nutcases.
We didn't unload gun cases.
We never made those faces.
We follow God, In God We Trust we say—
But in Self We Must Bust and Thrust, we live.
Forgetting metal turns to rust and us to dust.
Anything can turn to ash.
So why do we enacted so rashly forgetting so
fast our past mistakes.
Take a double take on which pathway you
wanna take before it's too late."
For love can live on instead.
Gods grace of love.
Saving us,
Giving us,
Life.

[Inner Spin Wheel]

Wish to jump into my mind?
Do you really?
Yes, really I wouldn't say if I didn't.
Okay okay, so what is in my mind?
An eating spinning mind that isn't ever winning.
Why why you say that?
Well I say that because once in you begin to
understand how much of it is a repetitive
haunting mind.
You start to see all the fun that goes on in the
mean time.
They say well, son you could not think about
such.
Not think as much,
Eh well yes, but you don't think I haven't tried to
stop.
You think once I begin my mind has enough
control to stop!?
It's like a rabbit that doesn't stop, it's hopping,
so boo watch out I'm in a goofy hippy de hawk
mood.
Yes I walk down memory lane all the time.
And boy my brain is insane with the train load
of thoughts at times;
So here we go, we about to jump in.
Once upon a time I thought about the sky, yes I
was also thinking of how I could die.
Sigh: it was a nightly king knights night.
Deep out 3 am morning crawling back and forth
calling the devil to come say hello.

High as a mother lover.
Yeah open fire mind coming over saying well son
you think you crazy enough yet?
Perhaps I thought I wouldn't relapse but man
stop it, I couldn't handle it, I collapsed!
Watch out we about to see a demon.
Wait what you screaming, you been dreaming of
me coming creaming.
Na-na ha-ha yah we about visions.
La-la says hellos, yes let's let it echo.
Echo echo I say hello hello.
Oh no, here we go about that night.
Fire blazing; sky star night amazing.
Fighting with self about which should be
happening.
Rapping or trapping.
Get it rapping, speaking the known rapidly?
Trapping, saying the nonsense that doesn't need
to be said.
Demons or Angels?
Devil or God?
Talking back and forth with super superior
beings.
Saying man, I could be king also, or not.
Tired up in my own mind knots.
Forget I'm just a robot, so it feels.
Docked in a boat to shock.
Locked up in my own self with super duper
engines spinning.
Feeling sinning winning,
Penning an evil devil up,

God coming, calling away such,
Turning your past ages away,
Praying ahead of time,
Love only be the new way of living.

Sit and day dream—
Hit reflections and say,
'"Sky light beam me."
Blame?
Blame me?
But why?
Why, because somebody gotta take it.
Open a window in the sky and see me crying
inside a hidden opening, dying, at least trying.
Yell in and ask why, why?
Replying looking in the passes mirrors.
You hear, it's denying you.
Retiring you.
Why, why?
Because you didn't try.
Wait why?
Because it's life,
Live free or die.
Cry a river in December.
Remember the timber.
Hear a real me verse.
Lost cold down in December.
At least this thought goes cold to the ghosts.
Next Thought
Somedays I wake up feeling nothing but myself
around me walking.
My first steps I step slowly and my engine starts

to spin.
Sin tries to creep in–
I walk outside and look up into the sky.
I see the stars, some days and feel this power
that's God sent.
Other days look up and see blackness and
darkness and feel the demons scent.
Hear the S sent sound in this message sent.
Some days wonder if I'm the best biggest median
out there.
Fight against it.
Saying I'm not hell bent, there's no benefit in it.
I wonder on it till I hit Wawwa and get a coffee
and water some days so the pain drifts away.
Send a prayer before hand to get the power to
not need one, but nothing comes.
Still feel this gun at my head, dead head straight
on killing.
Say hello to the cashier and send a smile and try
to make their hour be better and try and say
something thrilling.
I drift away back to my Honda LX and wait for
my coffee to cool.
See another X and see the XXX the 666.
Wonder why my mind is a tool set and wonder if
I need a fix.
Some days think on the darkness and get all
green lights for it.
Most days think about God and get all reds for
it.
Baffles me; makes me wonder if I'm some lucky

being that demons get to understand my thoughts?

Maybe I allowed them over the years and now they have all ears on me and know my face expressions and fears.

I send bullet spears at them and have a war before I appear at work.

I take the pitch fork faceless protection off and turn,

Going turning on the smiley face kid face on.

Try to say hello to a fellow and get turned down by them not feeling it today.

So I gotta take that and calculate if I should translate that as they don't want me to talk to them today, and then I feel me being the being of a demon for thinking such.

So I go on, do no speaking because I don't dare try and tare someone apart because my hearts here heartbroken from abandon-ness out trying to lighten things up, ironic I know.

As the day goes on I appear emotionless, within emotions going on mad crazy.

Go through the whole alphabet of emotions and become dumbfounded lazy within.

Because I'm sick of what's within, going on as my mind spins.

Hint hint, I wonder who's still a kid?

So I focus on Heaven and try to peek in.

Think on how beautiful it is once in without any problems of sin.

Then sin creeps in and my mind begins to spin

again.
Examine my mind and life and see it's not
perfect, thrive for perfection though, no wonder
the clock within always is sinking in with just
mouths ago I was out side 3 AM devil praying.
Seeing this recovery road may take longer than
expected, so noted for future record.
See how evil I am and fight against rather I'm
good enough already knowing nobody is
technically good enough.
But pull out my guts and a demon comes over
reminding me saying, "Hey boy you nuts!
You came on a holy book and made the earth
shake it guts!
Rusted down its nuclear protection of grace
once you had an erection on Gods amazing
grace word."
I fight back with swords saying that was back in
my hay day trying to cause mayhem, and damn
everyone!
That no longer is against me, so begone you
demon!
That's not right, I took a bath in some holy
water and meant it!
But then again did I?
Did I fully die to self or am I lying and the sky
light is falling and God is bawling allowing hell
to keep crawling over me some more because of
my hell days?
Or am I judging myself to much, starting to see,
I probably don't understand grace and

forgiveness—
But in reality I do, just keep having remorse for
my hell days, feeling I got a billion eyes on me
because of all it,
Putting me into high offices
Saying, does it really matter anyways,
I'm just going to be me.
Some demon comes in saying,
"Na na kid you just loopy and crazy and stupid.
You never were anything until we made you
something."
Screw you, I fought to be who I am, I know you
had faith in me because you saw what light I had
and tried to take it and turn it into false light.
We both played games and in the end, did I
really win or did you?
I don't know currently, but I sure know i'm
winning so far, why else would we still be
fighting here about this?
I still having blue days, feel when I'm doing evil I
still feel alive somewhat, finding its only because
I'm not fighting you.
Wondering why I'm being tested, read in the
Holy Book, that God doesn't test us, we test
ourselves by doubting Him.
Praying my faith will grow stronger, because i'm
tired of this demon fighting.
Blocking you out of my head thoughts demons.
Feeling when I'm doing right I'm the higher
person but feel this pain mixed in because I
know some days I don't live fully right.

I survive off misery it seems.
Feel it's evil beams come in and demons come in
and the fighter in me fights on harder.
Makes me play the God players card more often.
Feel my coffin coming in after me coughing.
Spell out hell in my actions some days and
accept I should go to hell anyways and get
carried away doing whatever I want.
Open the Bible at the end of the day to try to get
back in touch, and say tonight, yes tonight me
and God will boss it.
See Him on the cross and lose it.
Feel this guilt and melt.
Try to feel how He felt but can't deal.
Say tomorrow I'll try harder to fight against evil
with a happy face meal.
Invite in Angel Eagles, and say my name is
Dekle so you better understand I can live out a
hellish squeal you dumbed degrading demons.
I can write up a mighty powerful sequel overly
equaling all evil.
Because good vs evil can have many verses and
versions but only one wins.
Love does,
It wins.
So I win!
My evil twin try's coming in and saying no, no,
no only I win!
But wait who's the one in the lions dens: me or
you?
You, so screw you!

How blue you are doesn't even compare to how blue I can be, because you ugly boo beyond baby blue blue because your black darkness alarm clock alerted knowing your day is over.
Why you keep on trying to make me help you take over?
We had our make over and you lost.
Your ghost still tries on coming on following: hollowing out another hollering baller.
Me calling out bolder than ever about me becoming taller.
Broader than ever.
Hollering about life's pain.
Coming back into reality and still at the sink at work working zoning in and out.
Finding new things out all the time from observing.
Over see things and always pick up something rewarding.
Look at things frontward and backwards.
Slide side to side grinding out what's there to hide.
Riding the tide and seeing its pride.
Driving into its engine to tare it open.
Open a Pandora panda and eat a metaphoric banana and open a new method.
Get low into its depths and climb up its mountains.
Learning to understand what the Ever Lasting Fountain means so to maintain a mental state in my brain.

Come across as insane because I got a big brain,
making me saner than sane once you fully
understand; but understand I never was the
man some say I am, they simply just don't care
to understand.
All I am is love.
All I ever'll be is love.
By God giving me love.
Learned to run as the runner and never stay to
close to the edge of the thunder.
Gotta be in the thunder so you don't go under.
Been underground undergoing surgery till I told
the devil doc to get lost.
At what cost is it to be lost?
How much is my soul worth?
I always wonder,
For why must I fight on,
Fighting things nobody truly will ever
understand in this life, besides the ones who
have the Spirit.
Seeing even they don't fully know, so it seems,
for it all comes down to one huge picture in the
end.
One that has turned ugly for the moment,
knowing after any storm there always is a
rainbow, knowing the storm i'm comforting is
the Last Days storm, knowing once those days
are over, God Himself shall come in the clouds of
heavens and Heaven itself shall be seen.
Life still is filled with such beauty, it's
marvelous.

Searching out the positive.
Blocking out the negative.
Walking on in love,
For only then will the pasts song be made right.

[We Are]

We are the land of the brave and free who came
over from the seas.
The land who sought out for freedom, who
believe in something many couldn't see.
Founded in God We Trust as a must.
Thrusted onward in that trust until we busted
out into a mountainous country.
Many brave souls fell down into history.
Many felt misery to bring us such beauty.
So let us not forget such sacrifices made and let
our United States of America communities unit
in unity and celebrate this our Countries
freedom, remembering those who died and
bring that to the forefront of today's problems
and understand we get to live in such freedom
that many who fought for such didn't ever get to
see, but had such faith and believe in it, that
they gladly died to make such freedom possible.
Happy Fourth of July!
#LoveOn

[I Try]

I try to cry a man river and end up driving up a
wall of crazy.
Listen to a song and it takes me back to a time
and place filled with crazy.

Some may ask why allow such to come to pass?
I then ask how well you can remember things?
I remember everything as though it just
happened.
It's tragic I did a lot of black magic and
mathematics of bad vs. evil—
Used to be addicted, now done trapping.
Mapped out what's the best way to bring down
hell.
What type of bloody hell kid was I?
The worst you can get.
I can't forget I didn't do anything physically bad
to much, but mentally.
Brought mentality to a new reality.
So now I map out loves map quest.
I quest out its suggested suggestions.
Pore in the love from above,
Fixing course to better things,
Knowing as long as I try,
Love will love on,
Gods grace will cover it all.
Over and over if I truly keep on trying.
Knowing I'm protected by the Almighty,
That nobody can ever touch me unless God sees
fit, so fitting my shoe size to whatever size need
be, praying on God to keep me safe and
protected.

[Past Nightmare]

Knee deep down crawling around in hell.
Nobody can tell, though—
I ask for forgiveness and get hit back in the face

with a demon.
I say,
"Man, why do I get that?
Can you please give me another black and blue
so I can see the world again in a blur?"
I stirred a rattlesnake and raked in a hate date
mate, and shaked the wrong left hand.
But man,
Please oh yes please just listen!
I say—
I am committed to doing something good here
without sinning,
But wait I'm I fooling myself?
Cause once I am near a dear,
I steer the wrong way and end up at the end of
the day screaming seeing demons and asking,
What hell is this dear?
Did I witness this already before or do I live
every day?
Let me step back and get me an ax.
AC going,
Me growing flowing asking who dug this hole?
Snow is falling,
Coming bogging me down even colder.
Coming back being even bolder and older.
See my heart X-ray scan and run a brain scan—
See an evil man named Stan stained insane
trapped.
Mapped out to tap out soon but not soon enough.
Said holler boy—
Let me say that again evil twin.

Holler boy—
Yeah,
Holler and ask again why you after love boy?
Plainly playboy looking.
Devil deep down hooking.
Ax now in hand cutting down a money tree and
seeing me falling and it landing on me, me
fleeing.
And right before I almost die,
I sigh and say finally,
To rewake and say aww man, I'm still alive, but
why?
Sweet death in depth coming running
drumming coming bumming a humming a
dumbing—
Wonder if I'm a fool used tool?
Saying who's cool now?
"Yous, yeahs you?
Why because you're the fool haha
Yeah you so stupid."
I step back and ask was I just talking about
myself?
Of course.
Yeah of course.
Why wouldn't you be?
Deep down you're a genius, but also an idiot.
So listen man, I'm saying listen.
Sin city you tend to fall back into, so who you?
Yous a devil playboy monkey off key running
and having a hella boy key.
Keychain insane—

Explain please big boy who's me?
Ahh, so I'm not the nice one, so I say.
I try to be, but wait how can you be if all you do
is break hearts including your own.
Sweet born boy home grown to grow horns.
A rose bush with thorns.
Blush off a branch and say man maybe homie
baby I'm simply corn.
Horn torn thrown into lava and told to have fun
solving.
Found a bigger problem then I know how to be
fixable and see myself in the mirror as a
criminal.
Some coming saying mentally i'm selfish
Maybe hoppyfish popping out of hell doors way,
And becoming an soon angel.
I ask did you just say what I think you did?
Me a selfish kid, higher mentally seeking to be a
soon angel?
Which changeable doctor do I dock into now?
Wonder who suggested such a line as that?
Some wonder how my mind can never stop
hopping.
All I want is to go shopping for a happy meal.
A happy meal being a happy meal of peace and
love.
So much love, and so much peace and talent
that it spreads to all I come across.
Yeah, I tried stealing one.
Tried working for one.
Still so working for one.

For only the truest and honorable seek after
such love.
Went talked to the devil then the demons, then
God.
At first wondered if I was talking to a log.
Bogged down fogged out jogging running out of
breath.
I wonder if I deserve heaven yet.
Still seeing that my inner connector wires still
picking up the wrong radio stations.
God still coming in statically, but deep down
mentally wonder on why?
Deep down I can be nice, but deep down further
I can be a demon still,
But why when I try to be the saint.
Perhaps I haven't walked the fine line long
enough to be out of hells doorways?
Reason after reason says I committed treason.
Treasure chest check listed off to hell gates
enlisted.
Game face fisted.
But that's what the insane guy wishes—
That I end up in ditches washing dishes.
Mind spinning the insane out till conclusions
are found.
God enlightening more and more how I'm in His
heavenly books.
Wishing wheel spinning, me undergoing a
winning wheel denning sinning happy death
meal dinner take out to the dumpsters lava fire
ends ending,

So it can be away with.
Earth Darth Vader creeping.
Me falling saying soon I be sleeping.
Maybe when I rewake I can retake another look,
but who knows.
See myself awaking wanting to get up and
scream so loud that the earth shakes.
Saying some days,
"Hella boy back—!"
But watch out,
If I was back all would know because the earth
would feel me.
Why and how could I be so over powering,
I don't know, but it's why demons attack back at
me harder.
Probably because who follows me, controls all.
Is All.
God.
So see y'all i'm just me, but with God i'm
somebody awesome, but so are you.
Dark evil father keeps calling me—
Telling me,
"Stupid boy why try to talk to anyone else but
me?
Cause any you talk to, I will screw, and you'd
know it's true."
So here me go with my eh-O, oh no, should I
echo, let me go!
Play me something better.
Lay me something heavier.
Pay me something lovable.

Give me a high head huggable doable dumbo
elbow crossbow— Shooting a crisscross cross
crossbow arrow—
Stating letting evil all run hide and go!
For I found the cross, Jesus's.
Brain dead me fallen somedays, hell calling,
heaven yelling saying awaken, but me still
shaken eaten the bacon.
Stupid me be drilling deeper downward like a
coward,
Finding nothing awkward, but seeing
everything backwards.
Asking what reward am after?
Aftermath pathway driveway golden rolling
stone lonely zoning or straightforward heavenly
gate gazing star amazing—
From Gods saving.
Ahh, umm should I answer?
I don't know, but again I'll scream let it go!
Throw a happy deal in with a happy meal and
seal it with a kiss.
God's kiss of forgiveness.
Wish it could be dismissed into a missile, feeling
like It could go do something at least better than
this.
What's this?
Another nightmare so stares out the window
why don't you?
Why's you so blue with no clue on why besides
you wish you could die?
But hella tell a bloody tale why don't you?

Look into my eyes and tell me what battle cry
you see?
Yeah me—!
Why can't you understand me!?
I'll just keep on crying, so maybe one day you
will see, more souls still crying for forgiveness.
Especially mine.

[My Reality]

Some wonder if they would love to be in my
shoes for a day.
They think oh Sir Knight has to be some kind of
funny mind going on kid thinking only happy
thoughts, but haven't you already read, that's
usually not the case.
My past rots and taunts and some don't
understand how far down dark and low I can get
if I think upon the wrong person or past
moment.
Some see me for five minutes and think they
know me, forgetting I lived in the devils
basement for years and threw on a happy face
for smiles and giggles for miles and miles.
Inside my head riddles and mystery rhyme
technology and terminology run on and on
never stopping just plotting and hopping on
further and further.
The puzzles can never seem to be stopping.
I wish I could breathe one last time and that be
it some days.
But then I remember and realize this life isn't
even the beginning, and that soon we be

winning without sinning and no more twin
turbo nightmare demon listening trying to be
tempting—
Tripping, filling my mind with negative
implications of past wrong done committed
crimes—
God will be calling telling me son, welcome
home!
You made it; welcome-welcome home.
I give time & God it's wheeling healing power to
process.
But seem to get lost in the mist of it and the
ghost tries coming back out pulling me back
down into the hell hole telling me hella boy it's
your true home and your turn to turn the
tornado twin twister sister monster and cause
another blizzard and bring everybody down
even further for father darkness class A evil
calls you for goodness sake.
But I shake and say no, no, never!
Some think that isn't possible, that how could
you be chosen to do such a horrible thing?
Then I tell them I held the adaptor scepter and
took many steps towards such flaming fame and
played the game and sought out the devil, the
father and king of earth.
Awoken those early three A.M mornings and got
hands and knees down deep and kissed the dirt
and listen to see what next had to be done and
then begun my raging turning page gun and ran
to finish what was asked.

I did each task till one day the next was to
much, and I said no way never, never!
The overwhelming river began rushing and
pushing me on trying to kill me.
I fought and battled on—
Me God and angels fought hard.
I played the save me grace card over and over.
Found out it really works.
God will comes instantly when you start calling
with all your heart and life.
Began my homework workmen-shop stop hip-
hop block stock exchange change—
Disarranging its game face and turning those
fake happy faces into real ones.
Tried to make the best of it.
Tried to forget, but I can't.
No matter what I do or where I go evil stands
there smiling making it seem if I just come back
over all will be all okay again.
Knowing father darkness is the father of lies.
So nice try, goodbye.

Next Thought

Got no best friends, go day to day holding onto
invisible knowledge.
Wonder when things will start to climb; start to
fall.
I call above and ask for such information daily;
or please just let me fall over dead.
My head can't take much more of this nut case
raging, seeing as the times pass, and my focus
from my past fades off, things slowly shall get
better.

My Mirrors Reflection

I turn and seem to have the ability to go back
into the ages and seem to go ahead and feel the
coming pain somedays.
Look at the clock and see an hour past and go
into my mind and look again and another hour
has pasted and it felt like a minute did.
Maybe I'm falling into pressure and not seeing
the whole picture so clearly anymore.
But wait—
Let me state as it all goes on,
I carefully connect the puzzle pieces to find
clarity to it all.
I just go in depth about anything and
everything.
Thinking about everything.
I see brighter colors.
And know what collars I should be hollering.
Know what roller coasters I should be following.
Next Thought
Hollowed out a hiding hole in a holy book and
told everybody to watch out.
I found something that isn't anything.
That evils holy book has nothing to offer.
Beat up a drum beat to little bits.
Think maybe I need a new drill bit to hit
through to new blue cool kids.
Use as many tools as I have.
Wonder if I only give half of what I know,
Seeing I only try to give what I understand
myself.
I look into the mirror and steel the driving
wheel;

Out trying to find the next big thing to help
change this crazy mess.
Get texted self test texts by my own downfalls
daily.
Seeing after each past test, the past and my
faith in God is more finalized in whatever area
my self tested me on,
I'm only stronger, only more able to carry on in
love, in song, in all I do.
Because Gods love helps make it so.
Leaving, I'm never truly alone,
Just some days forgetting to call out above to
God,
Relearning the steps in life.
So I never truly fall, only stumble here and
there.
Seeing each day,
Life's puzzles are only getting clearer.
That Gods only getting nearer.
Do you hear Him calling?
Cause I hear evil calling on a thousand channels
a second,
But so do I God.
Which channel are you on?
Gods calling, are you answering?
#LoveOn

[Life's Hard]

Life is never easy,
But hard.
We play the cards we have been given.
We make the best of what we have.

We make today matter and yesterday the past
for today could be out last.
We laugh,
We play,
We learn,
And we improve to master life.
We keep God first,
For He is our motto,
Our hero.
We never forget,
But remember to learn from our past mistakes.
We take hate and turn that into love.
We know only true love only comes from above,
We thank God daily.
We listen to learn,
We share to give,
We love because we want to.
Life is never easy,
But hard.
So we try on the best we can be standing always
being the higher and bigger person for we seek
out to be so,
We our different,
We our Christians who never give up, but keep
fighting on the tiresome nights evil false light.
Placing right down to correct the nights
terminology of right.
Shining light on to all we run across.
For someone special died on a cross so me and
you could stand together and be family
members of something bigger than this world,

But family members somewhere so much better than here, and that is Heaven.
We all our princes and queens.
Life is never easy,
But hard,
Because of sin,
Because of evil.
But journey on to the promise land where life is incredible and wonderful where we carry on too
Where all you encountered and still encounter in this life will be well rewarded above your imagination.
For love wins always,
Love is all.
God is all.
God Bless Us All!

Now you are about to read about my past in a story format. As you read, perhaps you can relate, perhaps you will be able to understand parts of it. May this humble story enlighten you, encourage you, that no matter how far you have gone, Gods grace and love forgives all. That God is there all the time helping to guide you on, that all you truly ever need to do is call upon Him, and He will be there.
Thank you for reading so far,
#LoveOn

[My Past]

To step back into my past for me isn't easy.

It's filled with pain, heartache, hate, anger, depression, drugs, and sadness to the utmost, mixed in with pure evil. I hope you take what you're about to hear and clearly understand it was my past, and now my future is filled with hope, love, compassion and happiness because now God dwells within me. I'll start at the heart of where life really started to begin and where things forever changed.

At age 11 I was baptized, but I shouldn't have been, it had no meaning to me. See my Dad is a pastor, and over the years asked and asked me if I wanted to be baptized, so I just told him yes to get it over with. God and me never had a relationship at this point. I knew of Him, and simply knew a ton of information about the Bible; that after a while it became boring. I never could connect to it and fully relate, which left God pretty dead in my life because of it.

Understand the devil attacks those who people look up to the most, meaning my father since he is a pastor, but also their family.

I am a computer nerd you can say, so for me to get my hands on anything I wanted was very easy. One day I was with a friend and I heard this strange music, and for me at first I thought it was just crazy, but I loved it because it was so different. From that day on you could say everything slowly started to change in my life.

I didn't even know what I was listening to for a while, but I found out I was listening to rap, a song called, "The Real Slim Shady."
My favorite song became a song called, "Mockingbird," and a song called, "Beautiful," by Eminem. Among that I would listen to anything and everything before I ran across rap music.

I would listen to Alternative, Rock, Hip-Hop, Country, Classical, Techno, Dubstep, R&B, etc. but never Christian music, for the name Christian just enraged me for some odd reason.

I dove straight into all genres of music. From the 50s to present day. Music started to become my god and my religion, and I wasn't aware of that at first. My Dad told me to be careful of what music I listen to, but I was young, I thought about it and it's harmless, right? And after all, what does my Dad know?

At the age of 12 I told everyone I knew I can never make it to heaven. You have all these rules, why live life with rules always over your head? Everything I wanted to do; I was told no you can't; if I asked why I always got little answers to my questions besides, "That's bad, that's of the devil." etc. etc.

I thought more than the average kid, so adults thought simple answer would satisfy me; failing to realize the answers they gave me I already knew, I just wanted to know even more. Which what kid isn't curious about things?

Church members began to complain about what I was wearing to church, and did so behind my back, never confronting me, I never knew who It was, so I cast the conclusion it was all them. For once I understood they didn't truly love, but judged, I judged them all. Seeing all their imperfects faster than fast. They judged simply over something as simple as cloths, while I looked at their souls.

In so doing, I reflected back at my own soul, for it's what I do, see and reflect back so I can fully see if I understand and can relate. They asked my Dad: "Why isn't your sons wearing a suit and tie to church, how dare he be that way, he's supposed to be a saint." etc etc.

Some took it further and actually said I wasn't being the kid I should be, they forgetting I was still yet growing, still struggling to fit in. It left me enraged they would even be like that. They are not perfect, nobody is, how could they be like that and even take another breath justifiably?

For me at a very early age I saw things in a deeper sense having a deeper understanding to almost everything. Mainly because I saw beauty in everything. Saw that there was something to learn from even the smallest of things. I had to ask, "Why are these people looking at me and saying my wrongs, I can see five wrong things in each of them, how dare they say this about me? I'm only still a kid and they are adults? How is this far to judge someone so highly? I never judged you, but loved you until you judged me."

From that day on, I cast it out as unfair, for it was. Still to this very day I say so. It surely isn't love and isn't the God I know of. It's not my place nor anybody's place but Gods place to judge anyone. We are to only love and try to help understand.

I respected none of them, for they just were critics and critical to everyone besides themselves. I saw them as hypocrites, because they were so ready to point fingers at everyone else but never looked back in the mirror at themselves so I had to classified them as being very hypocritical, which I didn't see as being Christian in any stand point.

I label them as hypocrites, then turned that back at myself and realized I wasn't living up to how I knew to be a Christian either, so I begin to

ask myself why I was even still coming to
church? From how they are making me feel, i'm
already standing in hell burning.

I finally told my parents I wasn't going to go to
church anymore. They at first made me come,
but I stayed in the car, and never went it. I did
this for months, through cold weather even.
Finally, I was able to stay home, but I worked on
Sundays, so I had to go anyways to get to work.
Overall my Dad finally understood you couldn't
make someone religious; it's a choice to be.

In church school over the years, I was faced
with a few teachers that really should have
never been teachers. They were acting like kids,
having no rules of their own that were really
established and written down. I saw it as
chaotic. One day they would care about this and
the next not care at all. I was always
questioning everything and always found them
being very unprofessional. Perhaps I was asking
for to much, but I was a kid, a very rebellious
one indeed now looking back as an adult.

Understand just in general in the Christian
school system I never in my belief had good
teachers, it was like they all were being
attacked by the devil, and the devil won most
days. In the sense by their behavior they
displayed.

To state for the record though, I did have many awesome adventurous days, but kids will always remember anything dramatic and tragic in their childhood, so when I look back I tend to remember more bad days than good which I know isn't correct, for many good days happened, but during the time of it all, negatively ruled my point of view more than positivity. Thus it stands out more than anything else because of it sadly.

With some teachers being mean to kids, making even some cry, it enraged me. I always felt like the underdog, mainly because of having older brothers, so whenever I saw that happening, I asked, "Yet they claim God as who they followed?" Leaving very bad vibes with me.

You have to understand with me I am all about order and knowing what's allowed and what isn't, and fairness is something I believe in. Since some teachers never classified rules and brought others down by yelling, I made it my job to push everything to its maximum so I would know what's allowed and what isn't, and if the teacher was yelling at a student I would yell right back to give their own medicine back, so to take the heat off the other students.

I never minded heat and trouble, so you can

say I became rebellious in the sense if they didn't bring older to a class, I would give them reason to. If they didn't know how to, I would teach them how to. Throughout all my years in the Christian school system, I did truly have some amazing teachers, so don't let this side of view ruin your respect for Christain schools, but the selected few I did have that were bad, dealing with them for a whole year surely did engrave some bad vibes towards the whole Christian system of schooling as a broad when I was a kid. As a kid you take what you been through and think that across the board, for it's all you ever seen and known, thinking all schools were like that. I have personally heard countless stories over and over of young kids and even teenagers having amazing experiences, just for some odd reason I felt I never did, which is okay for in the end it all has turn out for the best.

To wrap school up, I went to public school because I hated private school so much for those reasons. At first my Mom and Dad thought it was a bad idea, I had to convince them for some time to allow me to go. Pretty much forcing my way in.

I loved it and became invisible. With so many kids roaming around, nobody caring who I was and they knew nothing about me, it felt like freedom. I focused on my school work and never got in trouble. Since I never talked much and was always busy with my school work, I was very likable by my teachers.

I stood up to bullies and put them in their place when I saw it happening, but did so secretly so I wouldn't have teachers drawn in on me. I never liked drama, but drama was always finding me. Finding later in life the reason why is I'm such a passionate person, that whenever I say or enact anything everybody feels it and knows it. Leaving I always spoke the truth and as a kid I never knew adults and kids hated that. For me I never saw any other way. It never really was in my DNA to bend the truth, I just told it as I felt it and as I saw it.

In private school for a while I was the center of the drama, not because I wanted to be, but I pushed myself into it in the sense fighting back and forth with the teachers, because I felt I was called to. As I mentioned earlier, I always cared for the underdog, for it is who I saw myself as.

If I knew something could be changed and changed for the better, every atom in me came engaged — mind spinning seeing how could it be any better? How could it be that much more suitable for everyone? As a kid, I just did this naturally. Seeing the bigger picture.

At home my brother and I would go back and forth, and the drama in that was crazy. It's not as I wanted it, for as I said before I hate drama. It's hard to explain, I'm all for fairness and justices, and I never was treated right for many years by my one brother. Now don't get me wrong I did a lot of immature things on my part not helping my case. But being the youngest one, you can get pushed under very easily. You know how it goes; Someone does something to you, you have to do something back to them, and that's how it was with us for a very long time. We were just very immature.

By 10th grade I dropped out of high school, it wasn't that I couldn't do it, I just had no passion to finish it. Which you will see why shortly. I did go and get my GED years later for the record.

My Dad for a very long while had anger problems, which now he is a billion times better; but he could sometimes turn into this monster and once it was all over would come back and ask for forgiveness. I can admire it now, that he would always come back and be the bigger person, admitting he was wrong but as a kid hearing the same message over and over after a while you started to believe it was just that. A message with no meaning. His anger problems didn't help in any sense with trying to teach me religion.

Thankfully after seeing him loose himself countless times over angry, I to this day never will allow myself to get angry, as a kid I did. I had really bad angry problems, probably because I was only following what I saw my dad do, but as I aged and saw it never solved problems rather only made problems worse I hated it. Promise myself to never be like him, never.

You see your Father and Mother as God for a while when you're a kid, for they are 'all powerful' in your lives. It's maybe why I after a while I started to care less and less about God.

See it wasn't purposely done I know that. That I started to have a bad view on God, seeing Him as someone always judging ready to tell your wrongs, my Dad did that because he didn't want me to head down a bad pathway as he did. He just never handled it correctly. He never expressed himself in a reasonable fashion. If he did his past ways of handling things would stand out in my mind more than the one he just enacted. He allowed his angry to control him, and for it, he has lived I am sure many hellish days. Uncontrollable angry invites the devil.

Perhaps if he did, the whole outcome could of

been different. He has always been more on a negative side than positive. Can't say I know why, perhaps because he's a lot like me seeing both sides of the fence. As a kid though, that can do so much damage hearing all the wrong in the world. A child, they can't handle hearing negativity all the time, with only just a little positivity here and there, and see their Dad get mad one second and then the next not be; then bringing God into the picture also. Like it's just asking for a kid to see a bad view on God.

Then seeing other Christians acting the same doesn't help either. It made me wonder if having God in your life made you judgmental and angry. As a kid it just how I saw it, I never understood the spiritual side of it.

With me being raised as a pastor son and having three older brothers and three younger sisters, and your Mom always at work and your Dad always busy, I slowly gave into the idea I'm better off without any of them; including God— so self started to become my center focus.

Mainly because my older brothers excluded me as the years went on, I tried my very hardest to be like them, but they didn't like it. Especially the one. You can say, as the years past on, I saw myself more and more different.

Always being the one seen as the odd ball. Having angry issues of my own for a while as mentioned earlier didn't help my case. Mainly because seeing your Dad do it, seeing it at least made effects happen, you learn to think that's the way to be. Then being pushed down by your older brothers all the time would make anyone feel horrible.

Thankfully as I aged, I saw just how anger did the opposite and now completely despise people who become enraged, seeing, they are the weak ones, the ones who can't control their own emotions. The ones who do more damage to everyone around them than anything else.

All I ever wanted was to be like my older brothers, but nothing I did would allow that. We had some good days, don't get me wrong, but in the eyes of me I remember being more pushed away than anything else. Leaving bad vibes towards them for a while.

By then my oldest brother was in college, I hardly knew him, just had this idea of who he used to be. My two other brothers wanted nothing to do with me and my one brother, him and me couldn't even be in the same room without some fight coming from it, usually verbal fights, which lead to actual aggression towards one another to the point it got physically.

If we weren't hitting each other, we would be arguing. We argued for years to the point we couldn't even live with each other but be 800 miles apart. I give him credit though, in the since having to deal with him being older for years made me slowly become fearless, so fearless that one day I told him, you ready to fight to the death?

Finally actually scaring him. That I was ready to fight to such a degree. See for him it was always only a game but me seeing the world differently, seeing it on a more serious side I looked at something like that as no joke at all, but an actual fight. He knew this, it's why he kept at it. He just wanted attention and all I ever wanted was love. In the moments of it all, I hated him purely for it. I'm talking actually hated him with pure passion.

Looking back now, I have to admire the deeper lessons learned. Making me fearless and ready to fight anybody to the finish. Turning me into the professional arguer, or now negotiator, in the sense ready to fight and discuss with anyone anything regular less what it may be, though I always believed fighting with words was more meaningful, it's the more mature thing to do, to a degree. Being kids, you could

get away with such immaturity, now respect
and common curiosity is a highly must.

    As the years followed,
I slowly viewed myself less and less because it
seemed where ever I would go, trouble would
follow. I would try so hard to be likable and I
usual was to people I didn't know but if my
brother knew them, slowly things would fall
apart. So I decided I didn't want anything to do
with Seventh Day Adventist after a while,
because my life already wasn't great and
everyone I knew who was Adventist I disliked to
a degree because I began to judge them more,
seeing as I said early just how imperfect they
truly where, not allowing myself then to
understand nobodies perfect, and the
compassion in me was very little back in those
days.

    Most of them sickened me.
Hell would be easier, so I told myself.
I see all these unbelievers and their life seems
so much happier. For a while I felt this free
feeling in it all. I dove straight into anything I
desired and became this loner. I was happier
with myself than when I was with others. I did
so secretly for a while, watched, listened and
played whatever I desired. My Mom and Dad
were clueless to just how much evil I was
inviting upon myself.

After a while all you would see is me wearing headphones, listening to music, allowing my mind to calm its self down from thinking, slowly becoming emotionless from the outside, but having a raging battle going on in my mind about all the wrongs the world has brought to me. By age 13 I was majorly introduced into society.

I saw what money could do and for me I became this gold digger, became this kid who knew a dreamer could make a dream turn into reality, slowly turning me into the visionary I am today. For a very long time and even till this day I have always been fascinated by technology. By age 13 I was working my way to becoming another Steve Jobs. I found this girl I liked, and through my all into her. Which to fast forward all that, since I was such a professional arguer and so was she it slowly fell apart. I tried so hard to keep things working; I tried everything I knew, but her and me I would like to say helped each other.

We were always tarring each other down and bringing each other back up, carving out each other's imperfections, and for me I loved, someone not afraid to tell me my wrongs honestly, sharing her perspectives, we agreed on a lot of things, and both of us thought from a logical standpoint, and for me I fell, fell hard because of that and she did too for a while, but her mother didn't like me, and it got complicated, but after a while I just got worst and worst spiritually, which I wasn't aware of, but reflecting back now, I know so. An evil seed was planted when I walked away from God and it was slowly showing forth.

During this process, I was heading for a depression and slowly started to shut down. I had all this passion for making money and making apps, and this new found hope of love that I thought It could maybe keep me happy, but my mind was becoming more and more negative that after a while it started to take its toll.

Things have always interested me, like anything you can think of. I have always wanted to know more about everything, because the more you know how things work the better understanding you can have, thus the better understanding gives you more knowledge, and more knowledge gives you a deeper connection to everything, giving life more meaning, thus a form of wisdom is formed.

I would think and think none stop on life. Always reflecting it back at myself, and I never saw myself in any of it really. Somewhat as I mentioned earlier. I started to care less and less about things. All I would do is listen to music, watch movies, get high and try and forget about things.

Movies allowed me not to think at all, at first, but after a while I could still be thinking while watching them, comprehending everything seeing a deeper meaning in it all. It was easy for me. Some say they loose themselves in movies, in music, I say yes apart of me does, but another part is still very alive and actively spinning thoughts on forward. I feel we all are like this though, some may just never realize it.

Slow music allowed me to think, and faster music did too, but it was harder. The faster the music, the better I felt because I would loose myself in the music. It's why rap became my favorite. I would listen and my mind would stop and focus on what's being said and meditate that back into my life for a moment.

You have hundreds of words said in minutes. Eminem rapped a song called, "Rap god" in 6 minutes and 4 seconds and said 1,560 words which is averaging 4.28 words per second. Now most rappers rap around 2.5-3.5 words per second and, 'Rap god', wasn't even around then, but I think you get my point.

You have stories being told so quickly. Most of the stores filled with the artist going through hardship, hate, dealing with drugs, sadness and talking about the game of fame and the inner game dealing with the devil, which many seem to never connect the two, or even see the two at all. Which is sad, for it's talked about often.

Now think about a depressed kid hearing of artist who also were also depressed, and how they just fought through it and made it to all these riches. And for you that's all you can relate to, so that's all you fully hear in the music. Not understanding most of them are also talking about the pain of the fame and all they did to gain such fame and the battles they have with their own personal demons in their lives. After hearing these songs hundreds of times, you begin to think maybe that's what you want.

At age 15 I started to write my own music, my own raps. Once I started that it's all I focused on besides my ex lover. See from ages 13-16 I went through a depression, by age 15 I on a daily was told kill yourself, kill yourself; life is meaningless. The devil knew something about me, in the sense for years he tried to kill me, so finally he thought of a new way to use me if I wouldn't give in to his way of killing myself. I saw everything upside down for a long while. After some time, my ex lover saw where I was heading, saw me as a stoner, a crazy bipolar kid who was throwing his life away to stupidity and even started to see this monster beginning to form, I swear she did.

By then programming and any other future realist dreams were gone. She left me, and it was forever better that way, for our pathways are different, but it through me further into a depression. Even begged for death to come find me to take my pain away. Opening a door for death to come, aka the devil.

For see love fills this void inside us all, this void we all have, and many don't understand that the only true person who can fill it is God. Yes, love can help fill it, but even in that, only Gods love can fully fulfill it completely, for He knows you, knows your all, and God is love. If you ever want true lasting love, go to God for it.

You can say I would see the whole picture, not just half of it, meaning I would see positive and negative in everything no matter what it was, but being depressed left me to hold onto the negative more than anything else.
This world has a lot of it to offer, so I saw it everywhere.

I slowly became blinded to the positive without even realizing it after a while. For I never allowed God to show me His beauty. I threw Him out, away, choosing to take my own way. Thinking I knew better, but also feeling I was cursed by God.

Finally, I was broken completely by this point, and the devil knew it. I was smoking a lot of weed by then, like a ton of it. Getting drunk whenever I could. I was high all the time if I didn't have it to feed my pain away I would feel life in this hopelessness. My parents could see it. I used to be able to hide my depression, my sadness, my emotions in all aspects, but the further I got in, the more I just didn't care. You saw it in my eyes. In the way I answered to things.

This angry from within started to form, this hate for the world did too, for everyone who ever did me wrong I wanted to crush, wanted to prove all they ever were was trash, monsters. I justified all I felt by always caring for those who were hurt by the 'monsters.' Not seeing, I was turning into my own.

I dropped out high school by then and was determined to make it as a mainstream rapper. I didn't care about anything. Didn't care who I hurt. All I felt was pain and hate, so I served it out to the 'monsters' I thought deserved to be ruined. I always showed love to those who showed love to me, and who never judged me, so to strangers, they always saw the best sides of me, and to those who questioned me, or put others down, I was the death monster, who would make it my duty to ruin them in anyway possible, for it was people like that who broke me, so I saw it as justifiable, paying them there welled served medicine back.

I started to write raps, like crazy all the time. Eminem was my idol, my mentor, and I respected him to the utmost. Till this day, no matter what anybody says, I admire and respect him fully, I don't idolize him like I used too, I just now can fully relate to him in all ways almost. Leaving, his soul is precious, and his heart is huge, and he faces demons that many just don't fully understand. He will always be in my prayers, and no matter what anybody says about him, I will defend his honor, and his legacy, and his legacy has always been:

Be you, do what passions you: push the skies to the limits, and fall in love with it while doing so. I don't want to say loose yourself in it, but I will say do so if Jesus is a part of it. That God, and family matters, and that evil is very real.

If you don't hear that message in his music, then you haven't tried to listen for his cry towards such. With drugs and demons being a a part of his life, of course he is not perfect, but nobody is. So for the record, I'll always fight for the good I have seen in him, but I'll do that for anybody. Noting for those who could take this wrong, of course most of his songs shouldn't be listened to, but for those who have heard him, you understand what I say.

I begin to write anything like he did, but added my life story to it, my twist to it, so it was different but just as deadly. It was lyrically complex to the fullest. Songs of love, mix with hateful painful dagger-full words of hate towards the world and people. Line with beautiful twisted words of hope. Raging on words about the end of all things. Hateful songs of pure devilish words of death. Ideas of kings and gods and money and gold and power. Anything you can imagine I wrote about in a beautiful poetic complex lyrically format.

You can say I still write in a way like that, but now I put God into it, taking out the hate, and preparing it with love in mind and the truths to evils truest realities. Trying my hardest to be the best role model I can to all I run across. Stating now and forever I will, I am not perfect, I will mess up, so look to God always, not me.

One day I was listening to a song I heard hundreds of times by Eminem and something clicked. In the sense the song was all about the rap game, how he sold his soul, how demons are his company, so I listen to the whole album listening for how he gained such power. See rap is like scrambled eggs for your brain. You hear so much so fast and the topics change all the time in a rap to a degree that you hear so much that your brain doesn't fully understand it besides the basic parts. Rap is filled with metaphors and allusions. It's poetry. Leaving ones mind to say then afterwards a million things of it own.

A good rapper can tell a story that's fully understandable the whole way through, but every rapper will put metaphors in a rap that only he will fully understand and those themselves in the rap and music game. Which I was in the rap game by then and didn't even realize it. I could relate to some of what he was saying and it fed me with confidence that I could make it in the rap game.

I begin to listen to music that was dark, hateful— taking about demons, turned to start listening to medal. I would listen to it and feel the demons within come to life. I would get this feeling of power; I would listen to something hardcore and then go rap, feeling like god, rapping masterpieces without even trying. Already I was purely listening to my demons, and slowly becoming demonized more and more.

By 16 I was a Satanist, knew by then if you didn't have God in your life, you better get in line to who controls society, who controls money power and fame. I played the devils game for a long while. By then I was working my way to becoming a mainstream rapper, an instrument of destruction to any and all. Whatever I wanted was taken, so I lived off hate and sadness and the purest form of hate and sadness which is dangerous.

Whenever I would rap, I would feel alive, and feel happy, so I rapped and rapped all the time. You could hear the hate in my voice and sadness. You would hear the demons within my voice, which is hard to explain. I started to freestyle and use that as my practices to warm up. I begin to be able to freestyle masterpieces. Freestyling is you rapping without writing anything down. It's you just starting off with an idea in your mind and creating that into lyrical format.

See as the years went on, my rhyming vocabulary just got bigger and bigger. Till this day, it's only gaining bigger and bigger, I just now use my rhyming skills in a different way. I could do that for hours upon hours. By then I was emotionless, and at any given moment could be in enraged, sad, happy, etc, and it was a switch. I could turn it off and on, but those feelings never lasted besides sadness and hate. I trained myself to never show emotions, only if I wanted, I went through a faze where I couldn't hide it at all, but as months went on and the more demonized I got, the more I could control it all, so imagine a faceless guy walking around.

By then I was demonized by hundreds of demons, which added to why I would feel whatever they wanted me to feel and why I could freestyle none stop so professional.
As the years past, I was less and less demonized, for my training was slowly ending, but at any given moment any demon of the devils choice could come by and come help. Which I never truly was aware of until later on.

I could look in the mirror and never see myself. I simply saw someone else, not me though. Each day of the year I was somebody else. One day I was happy, the next sad, the next sorrowful, etc. A lot had to do with me not fully knowing my self, or 'finding my self' and accepting myself yet. Which being so young, that is normal, but nobody ever told me that, so I never knew. I just thought I never was even present, that the demon was, knowing now, it was half and half. Learning also now it's all a mindset in a lot of was. A personality gift from God. As in, I was made to feel for everyone, so I could touch everyone, back at such a young age I never knew this, but of course the devil did, hence why he wanted me so bad.

Back in those day though, being so clueless to who I was, the devil knew how to push my buttons like it was nothing. To help you understand, imagine being told sad things, or being told anything that would push your buttons to make you feel a certain way, and not realizing just how much control you were giving away to demons by enacting and listening too?

All they had to do was suggest one little thought, and you could do the rest. Could travel down pathways that would only help make you feel whatever you were feeling. Till this day, this is a true reality. I won't get into my personality type here, but mine is rare, but everyone acts similar. And the devil uses it to his advantage all the time. Which I will talk about later on, perhaps in this book, or the next.

By age 17 I was an alcoholic, and more and more closer to satan for he became my teacher and father. I could feel him when he was nearby and hear the demons surround me feeling their energy. Which just lead to my trust in them more. I would go into the woods at 3 A.M to talk to them. I never saw them, but felt them, and felt this power that is very hard to explain.

I heard their animalist monster like sounds at first at night, but then finally just all the time. It's very hard to explain the sound, but it's a sound no human can possibly make. Just imagine a deep animal sound that is so deep you feel the vibration go through you. Having demons walking by my side actually scared me. Knowing pure evil truly has become a part of my daily walk made me know I truly was a monster even myself.

My teaching was almost over and I was about to be released into the media to do my work. See you first have to build that relationship with satan before he will give you whatever you desire, and you have to gain his trust and respect, and have faith in him, call upon demons and demons to build your army and most importantly be willing to be fully possessed, which I never allowed, which really was God respecting my wishes and never allowing satan too, which I thank God daily now for over and over.

God works like that kind of also, you have to build a relationship with Him, have faith in Him, respect Him, and in His own timing He will send you the Holy Spirit to work within you more and more. Faith is always key in any relationship.

On a devil side; I was taught to be so nice, so loving, caring, and so outgoing, but encouraged people that they can do anything by themselves; that if it feels good, do it, if someone hurts you, forget about them, ruin them. I was like a snake, surrounded by leagues of demons to help me influence anyone I was around. I was turned into this monster of pure hateful fire.

Now understand also, God works this way too, but in a whole other way; see satan has taken what God has made and has corrupted it to its fullest maximum. What I mean is, God will help you to be loving, kind, polite, to have patience, to have understanding and all the fruits of the spirit, and so much more than the devil can, but also will teach you forgiveness, and what to love truly means. And this process can take a long time. It really comes down to submission. Many don't fully understand how their pride stands in the way of God, it's horrible how blind we can be at times.

God enlightens your pathway; the closer you get to God, He will send His angels to help you, will send His angels to help influence all you come across, letting you know that you don't stand alone at all, but so connected to Heaven, that some days you feel perhaps a piece of

Heaven lives in your soul.

God through all my years of darkness would enter my mind at least one time a day. You can say I fought with God for years, nothing I did could I ever run from Him, which at the time made me so angry, so enraged, but now I am so thankful, because if He didn't do that, if He wasn't always by my side, who knows where I'll be today.

See by then my Mom and Father had hundreds of people praying for me. And God hears prayers, but He doesn't force anyone to do anything. Trust me when I say this: I have done things I see as unforgivable countless times over and over. I have hurt so many people, I have cursed God over and over, but His love and grace was always there, and still is to all of us if we accept Him as our Savior.

The only sin that is truly unforgivable is shunning the Holy Spirit. My days were reaching its limit. God finally said enough is enough. See in all my years in doing all my craziness, I should have been killed, should have been so demonized, that I wouldn't even know what is going on, but God allowed me to always have a clear mind. Near the end of my crazy days, after drinking bottles of liquor completely gone, I still wouldn't be blacked out. I would only be drunk to the point my walk would be slightly off. For see I was feeding my demons. Which in my case if I would black out that would mean demons would be fully controlling me, and anything could happen then.

Near the end: God allowed them to come closer but allowed satan to come closer also. See you have demons, fallen angels, then you have satan a fallen angel, but he has a lot of power, insight, wisdom and all but he cannot use it unless God says it's okay. Many forget who satan was, Lucifer, created a hair below Jesus, but Lucifer was created, wasn't divine like Jesus is. We can't say how old he is, don't really know any of that, all we can say is he is a master mind genius, and knows more than any of us ever will know in this life time of the past; it's why you can't face the devil alone, for he will outsmart you faster than you will realize.

The nice thing to know is this. God won't allow him to do anything unless God okays it. Which can get tricky once you think about it, because you also have to understand you play apart in it all, your choices do. But if you follow God, and truly follow Him, God will protect you to the fullest level of protection, that's a promise.

Look back to Job; the devil had to get

permission to do anything harmful to Job. God gave him the okay, and Job's faith was tested, tested all the way, but he stayed true to God.

For me, near the end, God gave satan full control, satan tried everything in his power to show me his power. I began to see black magic all the time around me. Metal turning into gold. Piles of stones turning into silver. Clear sky day, rain would fall only just on me where ever I would go which was actually God showing Himself, I never realized this till years later. Rainbows would appear, but circular ones and they would follow me, but again it was God, which for many years I never knew this, I always thought it was perhaps the devil. The devil does have these types of powers, anyways, I back in the day thought it was the devil, for I heard his whisper saying, "See you can have all this power, isn't this what you wanted?"

This freaked me out. I used to be able to smoke my weed and feel better; now I didn't even have to smoke much at all and I would feel scared, terrified, because I felt myself being fully possessed. Felt myself being pushed away and satan coming in taking over and allowing me to watch what was being done. See I was demonized already, but they never controlled me in the sense they weren't able to fully control me, because God never allowed them too.

I was demon listening, understand, you can be demon listening also. The devil has the ability to do that. It's why you should always test your thoughts. Should always think positive, and daily seek after God.
God now let satan fully possess me and it terrified me. I was being a median, and satan was doing whatever he desired through me.
It was during one of these encounters that I actually ran to God. Asking Him, "I don't want to be taken over, help me" God stepped in and pushed them away in seconds of the request.

Stupid self though wouldn't just go back to God as simple as that, so this happened many times. I couldn't put the bottle down yet; I was addicted. I loved to smoke my weed. I purely full heartily loved to rap, even if what I was saying was like candy daggers to people.

See a lot of my stuff I wrote actually 95% was very good and helpful to anyone who has been depressed or going through something hard, but 5% of had to be evil. If it wasn't, it wouldn't be profitable for the devil to accept, thus help me sell, thus have his approval. I wrote a lot of devilish stuff, but the mixtape I was about to release was only of my best freestyles I have ever done. You got to remember back to the Garden of Eve, how satan is a snake, how he will lie at any cost to win. I say this, because so will those who follow satan. For satan influences them. Remember that.

I just loved music and so many other things too much just to stop. God now is God, He knows this, so He worked with me. I halfway worked with Him. I stopped following satan slowly, within those very days, I didn't feel like I needed to get high. Prior to that, I didn't feel like getting high to begin with, for every time I would, I felt too high. Paranoid high. I started to feel like life is okay.

See weed doesn't have a chemical addiction to it, but a mental one; but see liquor does though. So it took me about a month to fully say no more to both all the way. I relapsed back time to time for months, always because I lost sight on God. But to get to that point one night I drunk over two bottles of liquor and was being tormented by the devil to its fullest, and finally gave in and started to rap some, at first I felt great, but by doing that, God allowed him to come very close, and I freaked out.

I actually opened a Bible for the first time in years, and just by doing that, I felt this peace. But I wasn't sure what to read, so I was like why not start from the beginning. After reading for only like five minutes I was like what is this, I know how the Earth was created, this is so pointless. So I closed the Bible.

I simply just didn't learn my lesson, so again one night I got to the point I was feeling the devil very close by after many drinks and hits of weed. So this time, I told God this is your last chance. I'm done being a yo-yo going this way and that way. I don't want to head down this evil pathway anymore, but if you don't show yourself in a real way I will, because I know at least I have an important mission to do even if it's wrong, at least it's something I can say I gave my all to. I will read the Bible one last time, what should I read?

Not even in a second I was told read Romans. Now understand I was so long gone, had 2 bottles of liquor in, smoke over 2 grams of weed, and like most people should be pasted out or blacked out by then, but God allowed me to be functional, allowed me to see he can help anyone at any given time, and most importantly, that He loves me for me.

I begin to read Romans, and it scared me, as it talked directly to me to the fullest, and I almost had to close the book. I was so shocked that the Bible could actually talk to me like that.

After that from that night I felt this peace for the first time in years, like felt so calm, felt I was at peace.

Within that same week I was driving, praying, and I asked God if there are still any demons in me to take them out of me. Within minutes I looked back in my driver's mirror and saw these three men's faces driving in a greenish sports car.

Now when I drive I am always looking and paying attention, a car wasn't behind me a second ago, and now it is. The faces I saw I saw for only 2 seconds, but when I saw them, it was like I knew them so well. It's hard to explain, but I knew it was God telling and showing me the main demons coming out of my life.

Within that same minute, I felt warmth start to go into my heart. Now you have to understand my heart felt cold for years, but I felt this warmth go into it. For me, it made me partly cry, and it's hard for me to cry, very very hard because I have like low tear glands, but it was God filling His Holy Spirit into me. I can say without a doubt, I walked and talked with Jesus for weeks.

He finally left, but during those weeks helped me to prepare myself for the fight to come.

The Holy Spirit is always with you, you may not feel Him, but He always is. After a month of reading my Bible one week all I was pointed to read was about baptism, so I knew I should get re-baptized. So I did, and I know the fight still rages on, that my demons and the devil try their hardest to bring me back to them, but now I am walking in the right direction, and know there is hope for all, and that all have the right to know they too can be saved from whatever traps them. Because God loves all and has the utmost power to do anything imaginable.

Though you may go through dark times.
Hollow be His name.
Many dark places may creep on in your mind.
Remember who controls Earths game.
Fight on we must through cloudy days to appear upon to those sunny days.
The number one thing that counts in this life is to be counted in those heavenly pages.
Rage on; rage on against evil must ring on in our minds and hearts.
The end of time bell must be rung out in the push of the four winds.
Our haloes of light must be shown on to all.
If you fall, get back up and stand tall.
We need to hold out our hands to help each other to keep our eyes upon Jesus to stay strong.
Our song must be steady.

Our beat and rhythm of how we move as an
organization must be ready with open hands to
help those hearts who are heavy.
All of us must be workers for God, only then will
you see effect in fighting the darkness.
Alertness and readiness and wisdom should be
your friend.
Understand the end is here.
Meaning, will you stand around and do nothing?
Or will you do all in your might to fight evil to
try to win more souls to God?
This life is a nutshell, the things in it will be ash.
Only the souls of people who choose God will be
carried onto heaven.
God loves all, but out of love will show his mercy
on those who choose not to follow Him by killing
them to get rid of pain and evil so the whole
Universe can be in harmony once again.
Never forget, we are not alone,
That God has many other wondrous glorious
creations beyond earth.
Look at your friends; and ask yourself: have you
lived and shown them Jesus by your actions?
Have you talked about His love with caring
loving softness mixed with kindness?
Will you stand and be a lighthouse for God, and
shine off his love by your actions.
The matter of question is all to you.
In heaven, I want to be able to look back and see
I tried my hardest to fight for God, and not see I
only floated around waiting for someone else to

do Gods work for me.
Each soul matters.
Each person if connected to God can do anything imaginable.
Will you be a fighter for God or just a follower?
God gives wisdom freely to those who ask.
God loves all no matter where you are at.
His love covers sins.
His mercy and grace is ever lasting.
His peace is beyond expression, besides the most comfortable feeling in the world.
Good and evil is very real.
Choose good, choose God,
For goodness and love only make sense to follow.
Let the truth set you free from confusion, and may peace and love forever be our motto.
In God We Trust Forever & Ever!
Live Free Die or Hard Trying Giving Peace to All is my living motto!
#FightOn
#LoveOn
— Sir Knight Writes—

The End.....till next time God bless you all!

Thank you for choosing to read another of my books. I hope and pray you were blessed by these words. Life's an adventure, and we are always growing and becoming someone better. We all have been and still go through life's struggles. It is nice to know we are not the only ones, that many of us face such troubles all the time. For more positive empowering words: Follow one of my blogs Via
Instagram —
@jonnyslifeview

@sirknightwrites

@j.loveforeveru

@swiftnewsblog
Thank You For Reading
May love always carry us on through
any storm that comes our way.
May God stay leading us onward
homeward to Heaven.
Let our hearts pour out with joy.
Joy in knowing the everlasting truth!
Joy in living with God in our hearts and
minds and soul.
#LoveOnForever